THOUGHT FORCES

Essays Selected from the White Cross Library

PRENTICE MULFORD

NEW YORK

THOUGHT FORCES: Essays Selected from the White Cross Library
Cover © 2007 Cosimo, Inc.

For information, address:

Cosimo, P.O. Box 416
Old Chelsea Station
New York, NY 10113-0416

or visit our website at:
www.cosimobooks.com

THOUGHT FORCES: Essays Selected from the White Cross Library was
originally published in 1913.

Cover design by www.kerndesign.net

ISBN: 978-1-60206-122-4

A fortune gained at the cost of health is not a real success.

-----from the essay "The Art of Forgetting"

CONTENTS

THOUGHT FORCES

CO-OPERATION OF THOUGHT

ONE aim in the publication of these little books, is to suggest how you can increase your force. In other words, how to so apply your spiritual power as to bring to you and others the best results and the most happiness. The evolution of force out of ourselves can be greatly hastened and assisted by the aid of others who similarly desire force, and who desire it in a similar spirit.

All of us on this stratum of being need force far more than we may realize. We are daily beset with a host of unseen ills. We live in groups and communities of people who are unconsciously ever putting out evil or immature thought. We live amid envying and backbiting, amid those with whom grumbling and fault-finding have become a confirmed habit. We may be compelled to eat daily with people full of ill-nature, cynicism, and peevishness; and of all places the table should be most free from such jarring and discordant elements, for we absorb with our food the thought-element most put out by ourselves and others with whom we eat. We may be obliged daily to meet and mingle with those who are making their bodies more sick and weak through dwelling always in thought on their sickness, which is putting in operation the force to make sickness,—the very force, or thought, which, if directed to the imagining of health and strength, would bring health and strength. We are of necessity often compelled to be with the gloomy, the discouraged, the despondent, the peevish, the victims of inordinate animal or lower desire, and the avaricious. We must be, more or less, with the vast mass of humanity who live entirely in belief of the material, the perishable, and to whose minds there has not yet arrived a single thought that life, health, and permanent happiness can only come through the knowledge and the following of a law which teaches us that we *must be* in body and mind that which we mostly think.

Be our knowledge and faith and attempted practice of this law as great as they may, we must be necessarily more or less affected by the cruder thought-element, alluded to above, so much about us. If we are much with people thinking error, or putting out evil thought, no matter against whom it is directed, we must be to some extent injuriously affected by such thought. It is as smoke blinding our eyes. If we are with the unbelieving and doubtful, we absorb unbelief and doubt. We see less clearly. Our force, or thought, becomes adulterated with their cruder thought-element. For we do absorb the miasma of diseased or erroneous thought as much as we may absorb the material miasma of the swamp or sewer, and then such thought for a time becomes part of us. Besides, we war not only with the seen, but with evil un-

seen. We "war with the Powers of Darkness."
Every crude, unhealthy mind using a physical
body, has its following of like crude and unhealthy
minds, without bodies. The more there is of mind
in ignorance and error on our physical stratum
of life, the more of such evil unseen following do
they accumulate about them. And the power of
this combined thought on us for ill is very great.

All these things operate against us, weigh us
down, and retard our progress toward a more
happy, more hopeful, more assured, and more
powerful, condition of mind.

They prevent us the sooner from attaining more
perfect health, more vigour and elasticity of muscle
and limbs. They retard the realization of that permanent healthy condition of mind which shall no
longer fall into periods of depression and melancholy, whereby relative trifles are magnified into
great troubles, and days are spent in dreading evils
which never come to pass, for the reason that we
are not then thinking our own quality of thought,
but that of the fearing, trouble-borrowing, and
needlessly anxious people about us. They retard
that growth of the spirit which shall bring us ever-
increasing clearness and brilliancy of thought,
bringing us success in every undertaking, and also
ever restoring and rejuvenating the body, and in
suring a perpetual maturity, and freedom from
physical decay.

For "the last great enemy to be destroyed is
death," and spirit is eventually to grow to that
power which shall keep and use a perfect physical
body as long as it pleases. This possibility is
coming to our race.

In mental and physical power, the race never
remains at a stand-still. Neither does the individual. Invention is ever on the move forward,
developing new methods to lessen physical labour.
Force succeeds force, each greater than the last.
In motive-power on the water, the sail superseded
the ruder paddle, steam took the place of the sail,
electricity or some new form of force will take the
place of steam. But greater far than all these are
the powers which man is to find in himself out of
which are to come results to him for happiness
infinitely beyond all that he has ever dreamed of,—
results which are to revolutionise existing modes of
life, and methods of action, but with a peaceful
and noiseless revolution; for the superior power
is never heralded by trumpet-blasts. It comes
always from humble and unlooked-for sources,—in
mangers, as in the Christ of Judæa, whose advent
on earth was one dispensation of spiritual power
and light, to be surely succeeded by others at intervals relatively more perfect; and, as regards
intervals, eighteen hundred years is a short period
in the life of a planet as well as in the development and growth of your spirit and mine.

To further these results, we need each other's
co-operation and assistance through the silent
power of thought. We need that all who are in
agreement with this order of thought, and who to
any degree accept the truths which we have en-
deavoured to set forth here, shall give, if fully
and cheerfully so disposed, a few minutes daily
of their thought to the strengthening of each other
against the ills with which we contend. I need,
and you need, and all of us who are in the belief

of these laws need, each other's daily co-operative desire or prayer to give us this much-needed
strength.

I have sometimes been asked the question, "Do
you practise, and live up to, all you write?" I
answer, "I do not. I cannot. All of the evils of
which I have spoken, I find in myself. Because
I can see them, is no reason I can immediately
get rid of them. They come in part of life-long
mental habit, and habit of any sort can only be
worn off by degrees. I can now be irritable,
despondent, peevish, or fall into other evil moods,
at times. I know the evil of putting out such
element of thought; but my knowledge, so far as
it goes, is one thing, and my strength to throw off
an injurious mood of mind is another. I feel the
need of more strength to resist these evil tendencies. I know that more strength will come to
me through the silent mental co-operation I
suggest, and if you join in such effort it will
come to you also; for then many hands will take
hold of the log, and many hands lift far more easily
than one."

So far as possible, such thought should be given
by each at the same time. We suggest that this
time be at or about six o'clock in the evening. If you can then retire five or ten or fifteen
minutes by yourself, and send your thought to the
mutual strengthening of all minds with whom you
are in sympathy, so much the better; but if it is
not convenient for you so to seclude yourself, be
you behind the counter, or at the office, or in the
street or the workshop, and you can give but a
minute of such thought, it is not lost. It is so

much constructive force sent out. It will meet all the other streams and rivulets of similar constructive element so sent out by individuals or companies, be they far or near you on this planet. It is a force for good, and will do you good. It is a treasury in which if you cast a mite, that mite is certain to return to you with compound interest. It will co-operate and act with minds in sympathy with your own whether the bodies used by those minds are known to you or not.

But the sending out of such thought is profit-able for you and all, be it at any hour of the day. We suggest as near the same time as is possible, for the reason, that, in so doing, the greater amount of force is gained, as force is gained in any effort when it is exerted simultaneously.

The simple measure here suggested—that of co-operation in silent thought or prayer—will serve as the first step to bring you in spiritual com-munication with such minds as will cheer, feed, and sustain your own. You will recollect that every thought of yours is a literal part of yourself, and when it is sent out in good will to all, it meets the like current of thought, mingles with it, and forms a greater current, in volume proportionate to the number of minds sending their thought of like spirit to it. You help them to generate a literal, unseen, silent power or force in nature, which is as real a bond of communication and union between you and others of like mind as is one of metal. It is far more potent than any material bond of communication, for it is a LIVING FORCE which will in time embody itself in beneficial ma-terial results to you.

Force by the same law may now be acting on you, but force bringing you mainly unpleasant results; for, being so much surrounded by evil or immature thought, we unconsciously open our minds to it, and send back more or less of gloomy, despondent, peevish, or other unhealthy thought. It is almost impossible to avoid this, since we live in a cloud of such thought-element, and our minds may be trained by life-long habit to give way to it. We are unconsciously daily co-operating with this order of thought. We now seek to turn this force into a higher, better channel; and it is turned into such channel when we, if but for a moment, desire the welfare of all people, and exclude not from such blessing the person to us most repulsive, hateful, and disgusting: for every thought of ours, as sent out, is a force in nature; and the more freighted it is with good to all, the greater is that force; and the more of good it sends to others, the more good through its re-actionary effort comes back to us. A thought is not an "idle breath," here one moment, gone into oblivion and nothingness the next: and if but once a day we say in all sincerity, "May the Infinite Spirit of Good bless all men and women!" we shall find, when the grand sum-total of all our life is counted up, that the moment so occupied was of all the most profitable; for the force we sent out in thinking this may have been the only one which penetrated the murky atmosphere of thought so prevalent all about us, and, reaching upward, brought down to us its corresponding ray of higher, purer, life-giving, and constructive force; for every thought of real good brings to us its like in return

Some of you in thought are quite alone. Though having about you families, relatives, and friends, these do not meet a large part of your being. Your ideas, if you express them, may be termed "fancies." You may be called "queer," "peculiar," "visionary"; you may have learned to keep these thoughts to yourself; you are shut up, and retired within yourself; you meet all those about you only on their domain of life, interest, and sympathy; the rest of you is ever locked up; you are as much alone as if cast, like Robinson Crusoe, on an uninhabited island; you are spiritually isolated,—the dreariest of all isolation; you are a stranger in a strange land, a foreigner among those of your own blood, and speaking your own tongue. Because physical ties of relationship are not the real ties. Those only are related to you who think as you do, believe as you do, sympathize as you do. These may be people you never saw, and of other lands and races. Your real relatives are spirits whose apprehension and comprehension of life and all it involves is something akin to your own. These, be they with a body, or without one, you need to meet.

It is not good for any one to live alone; that is, to live separated from all related to them spiritually. In such loneliness you are cut off from your real vital supplies; because, for both physical and mental health, you cannot live on bread alone, or any other material food. You need for actual sustenance and health the occasional presence of those who think as you do; you need their outflow of thought coming to you in kindness, love and sympathy; you can have this through the means we suggest, even though their physical bodies are not near you, or even known to you. You have many near friends you have never seen. Their thought is a necessity to give you physical health and mental vigour.

Permanent isolation and consequent mental starvation cause minds to warp and wither for lack of needed nourishment. It causes insanity in some of its many shades or gradations, melancholia and a host of physical ills for which medicine, or change of climate and physical surroundings, is in vain recommended.

If you separate a child from its playmates, or keep it entirely in the company of older people whose interests and sympathies are those of more advanced years, that child in time will mope, and grow dull and lifeless. It needs the thought-element coming of the companionship of other children, as much as it needs any other food. Compel a man of dull, slow brain, who finds his principal enjoyment among his cronies at the ale-house, to associate for years only in the company of philosophers and scientists, and that man in time will suffer in mind and body through isolation from his own quality of mind and thought, which is also to him a certain food and support.

You are under the operation of the same law,— the law that minds of like quality must be fed from other minds similar in sympathy and interests, or physical disease will come of lack of such unseen nourishment.

Co-operation hitherto has only been supposed possible by the bringing of people's bodies together. But, as is often seen, the massing of bodies in societies and organizations when minds are not in unison, has effected little or nothing.

The only successful co-operation for affecting results in business, or any undertaking, is that of the unseen thought-element coming of minds working in agreement and concord. No external organization, whether of politics, religion, or business, flourishes otherwise.

Such co-operation can be effectual when the physical bodies of those so using their thought, or force, are far apart, and (physically) unknown to each other. In other words, if you are daily for a short time sending out a thought of perfect good will to all, friend or enemy, you are attracting to yourself the beneficial thought-current of all similarly thinking. If you set apart a certain time each day, so to desire or pray for the good of all, you commence the more to methodize or organize this thought-current. If, now, two, three, four, or more of you meet, say once a week, to put your minds, or force, if for ever so few minutes, in asking for the realization of the highest, happiest, and most perfected life for yourself and others, you are accumulating still more of this constructive unseen force; and as so you continue to meet, and generate it, you will the more and more develop it into an organized power, and send it to operate in more and more channels for individual and public good, —even as the larger the boiler, the more force is generated in it the greater the number of machines are moved by it, and the more diversified are their uses.

As all humanity is in spirit joined together, forming one body, so to leave out from your good wishes the "least of these," is as if you should, in the cure of your own body of any ailment, leave out (were it possible) a part of that body. So to do, would bring injury to the whole; and so to leave out, through hatred, the least fragment of humanity, is to bring injury to the whole, yourself included.

As you thus continue to meet, you will, through this silent and mysterious power, be led to others, meeting for a similar purpose. Your force will then meet and blend with theirs; and so without any previous external organization, without any formal commencement, or written constitution and by-laws, you will find yourself in time in full communion, sympathy, and purpose with people all over the land, who in mind, refinement, and tastes are best suited to you, as you are to them.

There is to-day in our own and other lands, a greater average than ever before of relatively advanced and refined minds, or spirits using physical bodies, who, through the growing spirituality of our era, have been able to be re-incarnated. Because as opinion broadens, and becomes more liberal on the earth, it represents a literal element which has enabled a finer type of spirits to come nearer earth, and thereby to secure for themselves new bodies to act with on the earth; and the securing of these bodies is a necessity in order to acquire that degree of power which shall make the spirit free, independent, and complete master of the material. You, as a spirit, must have and use a physical body, and profit through all the experiences of a physical body, until such power is gained or grown to; and you must be re-incarnated, or use one physical body after another, *until*

you attain to a certain degree of spiritual knowledge, and consequent power.

Then, and then only, does your real life commence. When you have passed the period and
necessity of your many past unconscious re-incar-
nations, the initial point of your real existence has
commenced. Then the material is no longer, as
now, your master. You are master then of the
material, and, having power over the elements,
can make at pleasure a physical body, or any other
physical thing, to use on the earth-domain of life,—
a power to which some individuals have grown in
the past, and more are so to grow in the future.
Another result of this development, or evolution,
will be the blending of the higher spiritual world
with our material world,—the coming of the New
Jerusalem, as one of the scribes and seers of the
early Christian era expressed it, when people shall
live in the spiritual or material at will.

If you are of this order of mind and advanced
type of spirit, it is of the utmost importance that
you heed our simple suggestion. For, in so sending out your thought, you are establishing a bond
of mental communion with the like order of mind.
This will in time bring you to those who need you
as you need them. You need communication and
interchange with your like order of thought, in
order to strengthen and confirm you, so that you
may know that ideas, which for years have been
knocking at your doors, are living truths, and not
"notions" or "fancies," as you will know when
you find that others far from you, and for all your
previous life unknown to you, have been thinking
similar ideas.

Co-operation of desire in the spirit of perfect good will, though you do not meet physically such as desire with you, will serve as a first step to bring to you more spiritual power here on earth; and such power will go far towards saving you from the ordeal of another unconscious re-incarnation, where, through the relatively slow and cumbersome experiences of physical birth and physical growth, so much must be lived and learned over and over again with each new entrance into the physical life.

When you so come together in the proper spirit, having your bodies rested, and your minds as much as possible rid of daily cares and troubles, you make a thought atmosphere or element into which spirits like your own in high purpose and motive can come and remain, as long as you keep the thought-element pure. These may impress and enlighten you. You make, in this way, a place to which they are most anxious to come. They need you, as you need them. They will be of those very nearly related to you. The disembodied are not all independent of the embodied or of this world. In very many cases they need much assistance that the embodied *only* can give. There can be no sundering of the ties of spiritual relationship because one mind has a physical body to use, and another has not. The being the nearest related to you of all in the universe, and the one whose mental rapport and communion could be of the greatest use to you, may be eagerly awaiting the opportunity to come nearer you through the means we here suggest; and when these are taken, others will in time suggest themselves, which will render

C

such blending of related minds closer and closer, until possibilities are realized which to the mass of the present day would seem as improbable as a tale of "The Arabian Nights."

When you meet together, or retire apart, having chiefly in your mind the desire for the good of all, you draw and acquire power. That power can never be lost. It is not at all necessary, however, when you so "sit for power," that your minds be kept bent or strained on the purpose in hand. So long as the purpose is strong and uppermost in your mind, that is enough. If there be two, three, or more of you, you can, after a few minutes of silence the better to concentrate your thought on your purpose, engage in music, or agreeable conversation on any subject, so long as such conversation involves no enviousness or any sort of ill will, carping, or sarcasm toward others. If this spirit of evil creeps in, you will send the same spirit out —a rotten strand, weakening your invisible bond of communication with each other, and cutting off your communication with the highest and most powerful quality of thought.

Do not "think hard" when you send your thought of good will to others. If you are bent on a certain purpose, it is not necessary that such purposé is always present in your memory. Your force is acting on and for such purpose all the same, whether you are thinking of it or not.

Those with quick ear and keen spiritual perception will feel the import of what we recommend. It is not expected that our suggestion will be at first regularly or completely carried out. Though engaged in with zeal at first, periods may

come when such zeal and interest may for a time
fall away, when the cares or pleasures or interests,
or other phases of worldly life, may for a period
rush like a torrent between us and the daily regular
practice of a few minutes of silent prayer. But the
seed once sown with you will never die. Something, as time goes on, will, after all relapses, force
its importance and profit more and more upon
you. You will take hold after such relapses with
renewed vigour. You will realize that this silent
communion and mental co-operation is the first
step to your new life,—the life of your spirit in
happiness infinitely beyond the life of your physical being. You will in time realize that the
cultivation of silent prayer, either alone or in congenial and believing groups, is the true means for
giving you new life, force, clear sight, and self-
sustaining power for all manner of undertakings.
You will realize that it is the readiest means for
drawing on the infinite and exhaustless bank of
Infinite Spirit and Power.

"The prayer of faith shall heal the sick"; and
the thought sent out, desiring the restoration of a
sick friend, carries an aid to that friend. If others
join in such prayer in faith and trust, so much the
greater silent force is developed, and carried to
the sick person. If the physical body be so worn
out that the sick spirit can no longer hold it, your
thought is still an aid and much-needed help to
that spirit without its physical body; for all sickness does *not* cease this side of the grave. It does
not cease in the physical or any other life until
the spirit is cured of all unhealthy and false
imaginings.

You can excuse your shortcomings as to periods of regular observance; for it is quite impossible to overcome or change in a few months, or even years, the habits and tendencies of the physical life: and it is better far not to sit in silent prayer at all than to make of it a forced, perfunctory, mechanical habit. What cannot be done without heart, had better not be done at all. But you may rely that the live spark involved in this truth will never die out within you, though it may long smoulder.

To no force in the universe belongs such power as that of minds united in one purpose. It acts, and is ever acting, on all grades of motive. The higher the motive, the greater this power. It is used often unconsciously for evil. Its power is greater when used for good; and the power generated of ten minds for good is superior to that of ten thousand minds acting on a lower motive. But it is a silent power. It moves in mysterious ways. It is noiseless. It makes no show of open opposition. It uses no material methods of effort through tongue or arm or physical force.

We offer the following to those who may desire a set form of words in which to express a silent prayer:

Infinite and Eternal Spirit of Good, give us renewed power to overcome all our defects. Give us renewed spirit of good-will to all our fellow-beings. Give us faith, and make us see more and more clearly the law, the ways, the means, the methods, that shall bring us lasting health, peace, happiness, and prosperity. Give us perfect trust in the law of eternal life.

SOME PRACTICAL MENTAL RECIPES

NONE of us can expect to believe and live up to new laws, principles or methods of life all at once. Though convinced of their truth there is an unyielding, stubborn part of us which is hostile to them.

That part is our material mind or mind of the body.

THERE IS A SUPREME POWER AND RULING FORCE WHICH PERVADES AND RULES THE BOUND-LESS UNIVERSE.

YOU ARE A PART OF THIS POWER.

YOU AS A PART HAVE THE FACULTY OF BRING-ING TO YOU BY CONSTANT SILENT DESIRE, PRAYER OR DEMAND, MORE AND MORE OF THE QUALITIES, BELONGINGS, AND CHARACTERISTICS OF THIS POWER.

Every thought of yours is a real thing—a force (say this over to yourself twice).

Every thought of yours is literally building for you something for the future of good or ill.

What then is your mind dwelling on now in any matter? The dark or the bright side? Is it toward others ugly or kind? This is precisely the same as asking "what kind of life and results are you making for yourself in the future?"

If now you are obliged to live in a tenement house or sit at a very inferior table, or live among the coarse and vulgar, do not say to yourself that you must always so live. Live in mind or imagination in the better house. Sit in imagination at better served

tables and among superior people. When you cultivate this state of mind your forces are carrying you
to the better. Be rich in spirit, in mind, in imagination, and you will in time be rich in material things.
It is the mood of mind you are most in, whether
that be grovelling or aspiring, that is actually making physical conditions of life in advance for you.

The same law applies to the building-up of the
body. In imagination live in a strong, agile body,
though yours is now a weak one.

Do not put any limits to your future possibilities.
Do not say: "I must stop here. I must always
rank below this or that great man or woman. My
body must weaken, decay and perish, because in
the past so many people's bodies have weakened
and perished."

Do not say: "My powers and talents are only of
the common order and as an ordinary person. I
shall live and die as millions have done before me."

When you think this, as many do unconsciously,
you imprison yourself in an untruth. You bring
then to yourself the evil and painful results of an
untruth. You bar and fetter your aspiration to
grow to powers and possibilities beyond the world's
present knowledge. You cut from you the higher
truth and possibility.

You have latent in you, some power, some capacity, some shading of talent different from that ever
possessed by any other human being. No two minds
are precisely alike, for the Infinite Force creates
infinite variety in its every expression, whether such
expression be a sunset or a mind.

Demand at times to be permanently freed from
all fear. Every second of such thought does its

little to free you for ever from the slavery of fear. The Infinite Mind knows no fear, and it is your eternal heritage to grow nearer and nearer to the Infinite Mind.

We absorb the thought of those with whom we are most in sympathy and association. We graft their mind on our own. If their mind is inferior to ours and not on the same plane of thought, we, in such absorption, take in and cultivate an inferior and injurious mental graft.

If you will keep company with people who are reckless and unaspiring, who have no aim or purpose in life, who have no faith in themselves or anything else, you place yourself in the thought current of failure. Your tendency then will be to failure because from such people, your closest associates, you will absorb their thought. If you absorb it, you will think it. You will get in the same mood of mind as theirs. If you think as they do, you will in many things find yourself acting as they do, no matter how great your mental gifts.

Your mind surely absorbs the kind of thought it is most with. If you are with the successful you absorb thought which brings success. The unsuccessful are ever sending from them thoughts of lack of order, lack of system, lack of method, or recklessness and discouraged thought. Your mind, if much with theirs, will certainly absorb these thoughts exactly as a sponge does water.

It is better for your art or business that you have no intimate company at all than the company of reckless, careless, slipshod and slovenly minds.

When in your mind you cut from the unlucky and thriftless, your body will not long remain so near theirs. You get then into another force or current. It will carry you into the lives of more successful people.

When you don't know what to do in any matter of business—in anything, wait. Do nothing about it. Dismiss it as much as you can from your mind. Your purpose will be as strong as ever. You are then receiving and accumulating force to put on that purpose. It comes from the Supreme Power. It will come in the shape of an idea, an inspiration, an event, an opportunity. You have not stopped while you so waited. You have all that time been carried to the idea, the inspiration, the event, the opportunity, and it also has been carried or attracted to you.

When in any undertaking we put our main dependence and trust in an individual or individuals and not in the Supreme Power, we are off the main track of the most perfect success.

The highest and real success means (in addition to wealth) increasing health, vigour and a growth never ceasing into powers and possibilities not yet realized by the race.

As regards your business, don't talk to anybody, man or woman, regarding your plans or projects, or anything connected with them, unless you are perfectly sure they wish for your success. Don't talk to people who hear you out of politeness. Every word so spoken represents so much force taken out of your project. The number you can talk to with profit is very small. But the good wish of one real friend, if he give you a hearing but for ten minutes, is a literal living active force, added to your own, and from that time working in your behalf.

If your aim is for right and justice you will be led to those you can trust and talk to with safety. Your spiritual being or sense will tell you whom you can trust.

When you demand justice for yourself, you demand it for the whole race. If you allow yourself to be dominated, brow-beaten or cheated by others without inward or outward protest, you are condoning deceit and trickery. You are in league with it.

Three persons engaged in any form of gossip, tattle or scandal generate and send from them a force of tattle, gossip and scandal. The thought they send into the air returns to them and does them injury to mind and body. It is far more profitable to talk with others of things which go to work out good. Every sentence you speak is a spiritual force to you and others for good or ill.

Ten minutes spent in growling at your luck, or in growling at others because they have more luck than yourself, means ten minutes of your own force spent in making worse your own health and fortune. Every thought of envy or hatred sent to another is a boomerang. It flies back to you and hurts you. The envy or dislike we may feel toward those who, as some express it, " put on airs "; the ugly feeling we may have at seeing others riding in carriages and " rolling in wealth," represent just so much thought (*i.e.*, force) most extravagantly expended, for in its expenditure we get not only unhappiness, but destroy future fortune and happiness.

If this has been your common habit or mood of mind, do not expect to get out of it at once. Once convinced of the harm done to you by such mood, a new force will come and gradually remove the old

mind and bring a new one. But all changes must
be gradual.

Your own private room is your chief workshop
for generating your spiritual force and building
yourself up. If it is kept in disorder, if things are
flung recklessly about, and you cannot lay your
hands instantly upon them, it is an indication that
your mind is in the same condition, and therefore
your mind as it works on others, in carrying out
your projects, will work with less effect and result
by reason of its disordered and disorganized condition.

Ill temper or despondency is a disease. The mind
subject to it in any degree is to that degree a sick
mind. The sick mind makes the sick body. The
great majority of the sick are not in bed.

When you are peevish, remember your mind is
sick. Demand then a well mind.

When you say to yourself, "I am going to have
a pleasant visit or a pleasant journey," you are
literally sending elements and forces ahead of your
body that will arrange things to make your visit or
journey pleasant. When before the visit or the
journey or the shopping trip, you are in a bad
humour, or fearful or apprehensive of something
unpleasant, you are sending unseen agencies ahead
of you which will make some kind of unpleasant-
ness.

Our thoughts, or in other words, our state of
mind is ever at work "fixing up" things good or
bad for us in advance.

As you cultivate this state of mind more and
more, you will at last have no need of reminding
yourself to get into such mood. Because the mood

will have become a part of your every-day nature,
and you cannot then get out of it, or prevent the
pleasant experiences it will bring you.

Our real self is that which we cannot see, hear
or feel with the physical senses—our mind. The
body is an instrument it uses. We are then made
up entirely of forces we call thoughts. When these
thoughts are evil or immature they bring us pain
and ill fortune. We can always change them for
better thoughts or forces. Earnest steady desire
for a new mind (or self) will surely bring the new
mind and more successful self. And this will ever
be changing through such desire for the newer and
ever more successful self.

All of us do really "pray without ceasing." We
do not mean by prayer any set, formality or form
of words. A person who sets his or her mind on
the dark side of life, who lives over and over the
misfortunes and disappointments of the past, prays
for similar misfortunes and disappointments in the
future. If you will see nothing but ill-luck in the
future, you are praying for such ill-luck and will
surely get it.

You carry into company not only your body, but
what is of far more importance, your thought or
mood of mind, and this thought or mood, though
you say little or nothing, will create with others an
impression for or against you, and as it acts on other
minds will bring you results favourable or unfavourable according to its character.

What you think is of far more importance than
what you say or do. Because your thought never
ceases for a moment its action on others or whatever it is placed upon. Whatever you do has been

done because of a previous long held mood or state of mind.

The thought or mood of mind most profitable in permanent results to you is the desire to do right. This is not sentiment, but science. Because the character of your thought brings to you events, persons and opportunities with as much certainty as the state of the atmosphere brings rain or dry weather.

To do right is to bring to yourself the best and most lasting result for happiness. You must prove this for yourself.

Doing right is not, however, doing what others may say or think to be right. If you have no standard of right and wrong of your own, you are acting always on the standard held or made by others.

Your mind is always working and acting on other minds to your advantage or disadvantage whether your body is asleep or awake. Your real being in the form of a thought travels like electricity through space. So when you lay the body down to sleep see that your mind is in the best mood to get the best things during your physical unconsciousness. For if you go to sleep angry or despondent, your thought goes straight to the unprofitable domain of anger or despondency, and will bring to your physical life on awakening, first the element and afterwards that ill-success which anger and despondency always attract.

Health is involved in the Biblical adage, "Let not the sun go down on your wrath." Every mood of mind you get in brings to you flesh, bone, and blood of a quality or character like itself. People who from year to year live in moods of gloom or discouragement, are building elements of gloom and discouragement into their bodies, and the ill-results cannot be quickly removed.

The habit of hurry wears out more bodies and kills more people than is realized. If you put on your shoes hurriedly while dressing in the morning you will be very apt to be in a hurry all day. Pray to get out of the current of hurried thought into that of repose. Hurried methods of doing business lose many thousands of dollars. Power to keep your body strong and vigorous—power to have influence with people worth holding—power to succeed in your undertakings comes of that reposeful frame of mind which, while doing relatively little with the body, sees far ahead and clearly in mind.

So, when in the morning, be you man or woman, you look at what is to be done and begin to feel yourself overwhelmed and hurried by the household cares, the writing, the shopping, the people to be seen, the many things to be done, sit right down for thirty seconds and say, " I will not be mobbed and driven in mind by these duties. I will now proceed to do one thing—one thing alone, and let the rest take care of themselves until it is done." The chances are then that the one thing will be done well. If that is done well, so will all the rest. And the current of thought you bring to you in so cultivating this mood, will bear you to far more profitable surroundings, scenes, events and associations than will the semi-insane mood and current of hurry.

All of us believe in many untruths to-day. It is

an unconscious belief. The error is not brought before our minds. Still we go on acting and living in accordance with our unconscious error, and the suffering we may experience comes from that wrong belief.

Let us demand then every day, ability to see our wrong beliefs. We need not be discouraged if we see many more than we think we have at present. They cannot be seen and remedied all at once.

Don't take a " tired feeling " or one of languor in the day time for a symptom of sickness. It is only your mind asking for rest from some old rut of occupation.

If your stomach is disordered make your mind responsible for it. Say to yourself, " This disagreeable feeling comes of an error in thought." If you are weak or nervous, don't lay the fault on your body. Say again, " It is a state of my mind which causes this physical ailment, and I demand to get rid of such state and get a better one." If you think any medicine or medical advice will do you good, by all means take it, but mind and keep this thought behind it. " I am taking this medicine not to help my body but as an aid to my spirit."

Your child is a mind which having lost the body it used in a past physical existence (and possibly of another race and country), has received a new one, as you did in your own infancy.

Tell your child never to think meanly of itself. For if it becomes habituated to put out such thought, others will feel it and think of the child first and as a grown-up person afterwards, to be of small value.

Nothing damages the individual more than self

depreciation, and many a child is weighted down with the elements of failure before it goes into the world through years of scolding, snubbing, and telling it that it is a worthless being.

Tell your child in all its plans to see or think only success. To keep in the permanent mood of expecting success brings causes, events, and opportunities, which bring success.

Let us also tell this to ourselves very often, for we are but children also, with physical bodies a few years older than the infants.

We have as yet but the vaguest idea of what life really means, and the possibilities it has in store for us. One attribute of the relatively perfected life .o come to this race is the retention or preservation of a physical body for as long as the mind or spirit desires it. It will be a body also free from pain and sickness, and one which can be made or unmade, put on or taken off at will.

Say of anything that "it must be done" and you are putting out a mighty unseen power for doing When your mind is in the mood of ever saying "must," whether you have in mind the particular thing you aim at or not, still that force is ever working on your purpose. But we need to be careful as to what that force of must is put on. "Must" without asking for wisdom as to where it shall be placed may bring you terrible results.

Always in your individual aims and purposes defer to the Higher Power and Infinite Wisdom. The thing you may most desire might prove a curse. Be always then in the mood of saying, "There is a Power which knows what will bring me the most permanent happiness better than I do. If my desire

is not for good let it not come, for in its place I
shall have something better."

* * * * *

We need to ask for wisdom that we may know
whom to receive in close association.

As you are a part of God or the Supreme Power,
and a peculiar part, you can always estimate yourself as the very best of such peculiar part. No one
else can approach or equal or excel you, as you
represent and put out your own peculiar powers,
gifts or shadings of mind and character. You will
in time command the world of your own mind, and
while others may compel your admiration, you will
do yourself a great injury if you worship them or
abase yourself or grovel before them even in mind.

Idolatry is the blind worship of anything or anybody save the Infinite Force from which alone you
draw life, power and inspiration.

* * * * *

When we eat and drink let us remember that
with every mouthful we place and build a thought
into ourselves in accordance with the mood we
are in while eating. So be sure to be bright, hopeful and buoyant while eating, and if we cannot
command such mood of mind, pray for it. To ask
night and morning of the Supreme Power for the
highest wisdom (that is the greatest good and
happiness), and to demand this in that frame of
mind which acknowledges the superiority of that
Wisdom over your own, is certainly putting you in
the current of the greatest and most enduring health
and prosperity. Because another and better current
of thought then begins to act on you and will

gradually carry you out of error and into the right.
It will lead you by degrees into different surroundings, different ways of living, and will in time bring
you the association you really need and what is best
for you.

THE DRAWING POWER OF MIND

WE are through our mental conditions always
drawing things to us good or bad, beneficial
or injurious, pleasant or disagreeable.

There is possible a state of mind which, if permanently kept, will draw to you money, lands, possessions, luxuries, health and happiness. It is a
mental condition always serene, calm, determined,
decided, self-composed, and bent on some purpose
whose aim is lasting good, first to yourself, next to
others.

There is another state of mind which, if permanently kept in, will drive prosperity and health
from you.

It is only the very small part of what exists in
the universe that can be seen, touched or otherwise made evident to the physical senses.

The larger part of what exists and has form,
shape and colour, cannot be seen, felt or be otherwise made evident to the physical senses.

What we call space is filled with realities. There
is no such thing as " empty space." These realities
might be evident to our spiritual or finer senses

D

were they developed. As these finer senses are more and more opened, then more and more of these things or realities will become evident to us.

Whatever you think you actually make. You are making these unseen realities continually as you think. If you think of anything but for a second, you make that an unseen reality for a second. If you think of it for hours, days and years, you will in some way bring that reality to you in the physical world.

If you keep any idea, good or ill, in your mind from month to month and year to year, you make it a more enduring unseen reality, and as it so becomes stronger and stronger, it must at last take shape and appear in the seen and physical.

Of whatever you think, you attract its like from the unseen current of realities. Think or dwell on any form of crime, and you attract and draw to you criminal realities from the unseen side of life. These, the unseen, are the forces for attracting to you material agencies for crime on our side of existence.

When you read with interest in your morning's paper of murders, burglaries, scandals and dreadful accidents on sea and land, you are attracting to you unseen things of the same character. You connect yourself with a lower order of spiritual realities, and being in this current as you read with interest, day after day, you are the more likely to bring some form of these horrors and miseries to yourself.

These of the unseen, form a current of real element in the unseen world of realities. You connect your spirit with this current when you keep

these ghastly things so much in mind. That current then acts on you. You are borne along and
carried by it. It will then bring all the quicker to
you the elements of crime or evil. If you love to
read of the acts of burglars and thieves, you are
the more likely to have burglars and thieves about
you and in your house. You and they will be
brought together, because you and they are in the
same current of thought.

Neither you nor the thief is aware of the power
which brings you together. But no power is so ir-
resistible as one of whose action upon us and of
whose very existence we are entirely ignorant.

If you think but for ten seconds of something
ghastly or horrible, something which causes pain of
body or distress of mind to another, then you set
in motion a force to draw some form of this trouble
to you. If you think for ten seconds of something
pleasant, cheerful or beautiful—something which
can give pleasure to another, leaving no sting behind—then you set in motion a force to bring some
of this pleasure to you.

The longer you put your mind on any one thing,
be it evil or good, the stronger do you make it as
an unseen reality. It must at last, as you keep
it in mind or put your mind on it, make itself in
the seen and physical world an agency for pain or
pleasure.

The power to fix mind persistently on some de-
finite purpose, or in a certain frame or mood—say
that of calm determination, or to keep mind from
being disturbed, is not now very common.

Look at many people about you. On what from
year to year is their thought or purpose fixed? On

getting their wages at the week's end. Beyond this nothing. On getting a new bonnet, a new dress, a pleasure trip. Beyond this nothing. On living from day to day, or week to week. Beyond this nothing. Many cannot fix their mind on any useful purpose for two days in succession. It is this thing earnestly desired to-day, something else to-morrow.

Their mental forces pull a little while on this thing, abandon it, then pull a little on the next whim or fancy and abandon that. There is no steady pull or exercise of drawing power on any one thing.

These are the people who accomplish very little, who are always poor, and often in ill health.

These minds where fixed at all are often on the useless, and injurious. They will read with avidity of horrors and hangings. The longer these are spun out and the more minute are they in detail, the more they like them. They love the drama depicting violence or emotional torture. A vast amount of their force goes in this direction. It is a force to draw to them some form of evil. If turned in another direction it would draw to them good.

The unseen world and upper currents of unseen realities are full of bright and beautiful things— full of the spiritual correspondences of all luxuries, necessities and good things enjoyed here—full of beautiful things as yet here never seen and enjoyed. When minds here learn, as in time they will, to have faith in these existences, and faith in the simple means of attracting them, they will fix their thought persistently on the bright side of life.

They will come to know that the longer they

endeavour so to fix it on the brighter and healthier side, the more power will they have, and the less effort will it cost to keep their thought in the right direction and in connection with the right current, until at last it will become "second nature" for them to live in these higher realities, and, living thus, health and prosperity will flow toward them.

They will cease then to think so much and read so much, and talk and live so much in the crude, the horrible, the long-drawn recitals of crime, having learned that these thoughts bring them evil and injure their power for drawing to them that which will result in permanent good.

"Set your affections on things above." This upper current of thought contains the correspondences in unseen element of all that is good for us to use and enjoy, and more still of joys we do not yet realize. These are the "things above."

Those of horror, ghastliness, crime, and misery on which now so much of people's affections or thought is set, are "things below."

Evil of any sort is only to be thought of and dealt with long enough to remedy it. One remains in a cesspool no longer than is necessary to bail out its contents. You want to get your cold, your pain, your last sprained ankle, or the last injustice done you by another out of your mind as soon as you can and not keep making it over and over again, through ever thinking it, brooding over it, and telling it to others whenever you get a chance.

Such mood of mind may become habitual "second nature," and a power for drawing poverty and ill health.

Constant contact with crime, or misery with ill of any kind, or even the thought of it, will at last beget an unnatural and unhealthy appetite for it. So that at last people would rather talk at the breakfast table of sickness and death-bed scenes than of health, or of crime and horrors than of things cheerful, peaceable and pleasant.

All such talk and thought dwelling in misery injures your power for drawing good things to you. It is a direct means for taking money from your purse and health from your body.

Living ever in the thought of sickness will surely bring sickness to you.

*　　*　　*　　*　　*

You will be the more healthy for living as much as you can in the thought and the surroundings of healthy things. You will be the stronger for living in the thought and being in the physical surrounding of strong things—strong animals—strong and vigorous men and women. A circus with its skilled riders, its acrobats and tumblers, and its audience with care for a time off their minds and smiles in their faces, is a far healthier place, and connects one with a healthier thought current, than a dissecting room or the poring over a book devoted to the recital of any form of suffering or disease.

What we call the drawing power of mind is not that of longing for things. Longing implies impatience, because they do not come as soon as we desire. The impatient state of mind will either drive what you desire from you or delay its advance. When your thought takes this form, " I want the thing desired now—right now; I'm tired of waiting; I can't stand waiting any longer; I'm sick and tired of waiting," you are in the wrong mood.

You are then using your force in scolding or grieving or finding fault, because what you desire does not come. When you scold or complain or grieve, because the things you desire do not come, your force is set upon that scolding or grieving, and is not working to bring them to you. It is analogous to the man who, in a fit of rage, should tear his wagon to pieces, because it is stuck in the mire.

The force he used to tear it to pieces might have drawn it out.

The force of mind you need to put out to draw good things to you lies in that mood, which says, continually and calmly: "I must have these things; I am going to have them, provided that a Wisdom greater than mine sees that it will not work me injury to have them."

It must be a mental state of serenity and determination decided and positive, but never angered or impatient, or anxious or worrying.

So that you keep your mind in the proper drawing mood, you need not have in mind continually the thing you desire. It is the state of mind that draws money and things desirable, and not the constant recollection of the special thing desired.

When you can put your mind in this mood and keep it there, when for instance you say to yourself calmly and deliberately "I am going to travel and see the world abroad," you can forget for a time that special purpose, and employ and enjoy yourself in the other efforts, without retarding at all the power which will be working to send you abroad.

You need only to have the mood of calm, unruffled determination and decision connected with your determination to travel or any other aim which recurs to your mind.

You lessen this drawing power for good when you get angry or irritable; you increase it then for evil. You lessen it for good through becoming discouraged or despondent. You set it then the wrong way and for evil. You lessen it for good through hurried states of mind.

To covet the property of another person—to cumber the mind with schemes to get property through inheritance of another—to feel anxiety, envy and jealousy of others who may share in such property or who may seem likely to get the whole of it—to set longing and envious eyes on another's lands, houses, carriages, horses and other evidences of material wealth—to commence calculating on being brought into any degree of association with a rich man or woman, and how you may gain or wheedle, or so become a favourite of such person as to induce him or her to give you of their wealth, all this brings on a state of mind retarding your connection with the greatest drawing power. It brings to you a current of low, grovelling and narrow thought. It is loss also to allow yourself to drift into the petty prejudices of people concerning others—to take sides even in thought in petty quarrels.

You lose power by engaging with others in any conversation on a plane of motive and sentiment lower than your own, such as tattle, sarcastic remarks on the failings of others, fault finding with affairs which do not concern you, and unwarrantable inquiry and ferreting out others' private affairs.

You put out in so doing, thought forces which are opposed to and which will destroy or retard the effect of your higher and more powerful attitude of mind toward all mankind—an outflow of thought which deals only with the best in others; sees as little as possible of their thoughts; speaks as little as possible concerning them, and sends them in thought only good-will from which you will fight off every shade of malice, envy and jealousy—thoughts now so dominant in our stratum of life and which will thrust themselves in our minds at every opportunity.

You want power to gain the highest health, the greatest success in business, and the growth of your spirit into possibilities not now to be realized. Nothing so much weakens you in every way as descending in thought and talk to ill-natured and ferreting gossip. You descend then to the world of failure and ill health. You clothe yourself then in an actual thought-robe or envelope of weakness— the robes now worn by so many, who ascribe their ill health or non-success to any and everything but this the real cause.

Keep away as much as you can from despondent, reckless and purposeless people, and you will keep your drawing power at its best. You will then not lessen it through adulteration by absorption of their discouraged, undecided, purposeless thoughts.

If of necessity you are thrown in their company,

make up your mind beforehand that you will not absorb any of their thought. Then you put on a positive protective armour against such absorption.

If you give a great deal of your sympathy to those who do not believe in these ideas; if you make their troubles your troubles and their cares your cares, you lessen your drawing power for the best and increase it for the worst. For then you absorb these doubts and other defects of mind. You mix up your faith with their lack of faith. You cripple your decision with their possible in-decision.

Speak of your purposes only to those of whose friendship you are very sure—only to those who are not envious and who really wish you to have your desire.

* * * * *

Temperance and moderation in the use of all things, and in the play of all emotion, is very necessary to the attainment of the most powerful drawing frame of mind. But asceticism and ex-treme self-denial in anything only lessen this drawing power. For all asceticism creates un-natural longings. Then the force of mind is placed on what nature is starved of and will long for, and sets its thought or force upon.

Of anything which annoys you, make up your mind that it shall not annoy you. This decision will increase the drawing power of your mind. But if in mind you give way to annoyances, and do not resist them, you increase their power to annoy you.

You bring on also by this mental condition more and more annoyances.

You lessen also your force for drawing things to you. Or in other words you use that same force to draw annoying things to you.

Resist the devil and he will flee from you.

A disagreeable habit in another person, and impertinence or rudeness in another, a creaking door, anything in the working of the physical world about us, if we do not set our minds against its annoying us, will grow more and more upon us. It will master us. All these things represent the devil to be resisted.

When we allow ourselves to be annoyed by any person we are ruled by that person. For if we cannot abide their presence in a room, then that person drives us from that room. If we cannot be agreeable to others with that person in our presence, then that person governs our speech and makes us silent and sulky.

But when this resisting power is used, and we endeavour to turn our mind from the annoyance, we shall be carried at last beyond the reach of all annoying things. That is the real power for driving from us whatever annoys us.

I do not here imply that the habit of being easily annoyed or of non-resistance to annoyance, or the habit and love of reading and living mentally in scenes of misery or any other mental habit which lessens our power, can be immediately broken off. That is all but impossible. No mental habit, the growth of years, can be suddenly changed.

How, then, can it be changed?

By not trying too hard to change it. By not becoming impatient on finding yourself unconsciously reverting to the state of mind you wish to get rid of. For impatience at anything is force employed in anger, because matters do not change as quickly as you wish, and that is so much force lost to your drawing power. You can in this way hurt yourself as much when the motive is good as when it is bad.

It will increase your drawing power to *feel* the real need of the thing you set your mind upon. There is a great difference between wanting things and needing things. Some people want everything they set their eyes on, when they need but few of those things at a time. You may need warm garments for winter. You may want things which may have no use during winter. Now the need for serviceable clothing is imperative. For other things the need may not be imperative, though they have their place and use in good time. If you feel the need of the thing you set your mind upon, you increase the force of your demand for it. This increases your drawing power, provided, as we must say again, your demand is made in the mood of decision and patience, and does not use itself up in the mood of impatience, because the thing demanded does not immediately come.

There are two ways of saying " I must have the better things desired." To say " I must," or " I demand it," in the mood of ugliness or irascibility, carries little or no power to bring the thing demanded. But a great deal of drawing power is set upon the thing demanded when you say, " I demand this special thing because I need it; because it is right I should have it; because I feel that my ability to benefit first, myself, and next others will be increased by it."

This is the mood to be permanently maintained from month to month and year to year, until at last it becomes a part of yourself, and you carry such frame of mind whether you do it consciously or not.

If you feel that there Is truth in my assertions, then the seed of conviction is sown in your mind. That seed, that idea, that force will do the work for you. You need in a sense do but little. That truth will take deeper and deeper root. It will grow and increase; you will find yourself gradu ally changing for the better. You will have less and less inclination to live in the grim and ghastly as you realize more and more the danger of so doing. Better still, you will turn away more and more from the racks and slaughter-pens of a lower life as you realize more and more the power, the pleasure and the profit of holding ever in your thought things cheerful, bright, gay and innocent.

When you acquire this power, or in other words get your drawing force turned in the right direction (it is always working in some direction), you will know that it is all yours. No one can take it from you. It must also be ever on the increase; as it increases its force, it is increasing for ever.

When it is working in the right direction to bring you health, fortune and success in all you undertake, you depend on no one but yourself and the Supreme Power. You lean on no one. You will feel that you have the power within to accom- plish all you undertake. You will not then seek fortune by marrying merely for money. Or by waiting for rich relatives to die. Or by pandering in any way to the rich and powerful. Your body also will by degrees grow stronger, more healthy, more attractive. For you are then in the current which can carry you beyond the realm of disease.

Permanent peace and tranquillity of mind are the proofs that this power is working in the right direction for you.

There may be occasional intervals of mental disturbance. At times the force may return in its old direction. This is the effort of the old habit, the material mind, to resume its sway. Such disturbances must become less and less violent and of shorter and shorter duration, because your higher promptings or spiritual mind is the greater power, and must always subdue the lower.

The Oriental "Adept" or Fakir has this power to a limited extent, but he places it on purposes which, though wonderful from their novelty, are relatively of little use to him or others.

The basis on which he acts lies in the holding of forces in himself and gathering them also from outside sources by a permanently calm, unruffled, deliberate and undisturbed mental state of mind.

Can all attain to this drawing power?

Those who can have faith in it will reverse this same force now, possibly, bringing them poverty, sickness and evil, and turn it in the direction of bringing them good. All will not have faith. These will go on as before, using their minds blindly to attract the evil and suffer from it. All must have this power in some existence. All may not reach it in this physical existence, but will in some future one.

If you are alone in the world and lack congenial association, the mood of calm demand based for all things demanded on a continual silent desire or prayer, to be led by a higher and diviner wisdom than our own, will draw to you in time that association which is the best for you.

BURIED TALENTS

IF a girl has a distaste for "housework," if she has no aptitude for washing, scouring, cooking and sweeping, if she does not show the ordinary signs and proclivities for filling the position which the world accords to so many girls, that of the "good housekeeper," let her alone. Be sure that some power within her needs time and rest to grow. You do not make matters any better by forcing her to occupations for which she has no inclination. You are probably making matters much worse. You are developing an indifferent "house-wife," and starving possibly the soul of a woman of great ability, in some direction.

Rank heresy! Nonsense! you cry. "Every girl should be taught to bake, brew, boil, sweep, scrub and how to 'keep house.' She should not be brought up in idleness."

Very good, drive your idle child to work, vex her soul with pots and pans. Ten or fifteen years hence, look upon her and see if she is an honour to your strict training. Many are the broken down creatures to-day who might have "amounted to something," had the talent or talents given to them, been allowed time and rest in which to grow and be recognized and fostered when they put forth their first buds of promise. You cannot drive a quality, a power, a talent in upon itself, without risk of dreadful results. Would you attempt to hammer back the apple bud and insist that it be a pear blossom? That is the rule of the world in thousands of cases. The bud of the youthful artist is discouraged, the rising genius repressed perhaps by the parent. Why? "Oh, artists are such a poor lot. They do not, save in exceptional cases, make money." True. And for such reason it is sometimes, that the parents take the child's talent and bury it for him, or her.

Power and talent grow in repose. The solution of mineral producing the finest crystallization, needs to be kept perfectly quiet while the new combination is forming. The best fruitage of mind whether of invention, art, science, or sentiment, must form under similar conditions. Your "original thinker" develops best while he is apparently idle. "Industry" in what is called "literary work," often makes "hacks" of race horses. Every man and every woman contain in themselves the elements and powers in embryo of entire self-reliance. Every individual should so base himself in his mind. You should say continually to yourself, "though I have not the power to carry out my design to-day, still I am ever growing up to that power. If I lean or depend for help to-day, still it is my aspiration to be independent of such dependency as soon as possible."

Dependency on somebody or something is one

of the unconscious errors in thought most prevalent to day. Theology has taught that we are
" nothing without God." So we are. But God or
the Infinite Spirit of good and power is everywhere,
and we have the glorious and, as yet, unappreci-
ated power of ever calling to us and adding etern-
ally to ourselves more and more of this spirit or
element.

God or the Infinite Spirit of good "works in us
and through us." We are all parts of God, and
each individual as such part, is ever glorifying God
by gaining more and more Godliness. That is,
more and more power for doing. We must hold
the thought in our minds that we have more of
this power to-day than we had yesterday. We must
cut loose more and more from the idea of a dependency on anyone or any power, save the power we
can ever call to ourselves. Every individual is an
empire ever increasing in power.

" But are we not dependent on others in every
phase of life?" may be asked. "How should we
live did not others prepare our food, build our
houses, wash our clothing, and minister to our
many needs?" We answer, it is a law of nature
that the more we wisely try to help ourselves, the
more do we help others, and thereby get help from
them. Wisdom makes effort to gain perfect health
and a balanced mind. The mere possession of
these alone is a benefit to all with whom we come
in contact and many more. If your spirit is power
ful and healthy it will send its invigorating forces
to people far from you. A spirit which has reached
the consciousness that it is through prayer, or the
law of demand, ever calling to itself new forces

E

from the exhaustless source of force, and nevei losing an atom of that force, so called to it, is a benefit to thousands it may never see with the physical eye.

It is sending of its force to every person of whom it thinks. It is as a sun warming into life all on whom it shines, even as our sun begets life out of the rugged rock on which its rays fall.

As you increase in patience, in exactness, in decision, in method, in neatness, in self-control, in all that goes to make of yourself a relatively perfect organized being, do these qualities flow from you to others, and as they increase in these will they flow back from those they benefit to you. If you send this quality of thought to them from the impulse of love or desire to help, so will they respond in time, and send the same quality back to you through the resistless impulse of love and gratitude. You cannot help others without being helped yourself. You cannot send out helpful thought to others without getting from them in return helpful thought so far as they have ability to give it. You cannot injure others without being injured yourself. You cannot send any shade of evil thought to others without injury to yourself. If those to whom you send such character of evil thought meet it and turn it aside by the thought of goodwill to you, your thought will return to you. Self-dependence brings to you the very result unwisely sought by dependence. The person who leans on you and depends on you for everything must tire you out at last. You will see eventually how great an injustice it is to allow any person so to depend. It cripples their own capacity for independence. It retards the strengthening of that power through exercise by which they could call to themselves more of any quality out of the elements, or, in other words, out of the boundless realm of Infinite Spirit or Force. You are offering yourself as a crutch to a person who has sound limbs. To encourage dependency in another is to strengthen their delusion in their own weakness. It is teaching them to be everlasting borrowers when they have a bank of their own. It is often as the lending to them of means which they cannot wholly appropriate or use to best advantage, while others might be greatly benefited by such means and repay you a far better interest.

It is right to expect return for what we give. It is right because it is a necessity. If you are ever giving another of the richness of your superior thought; if you are always planning and working for the entertainment and pleasure of some person who takes all you give and has for you little or no power to entertain you in return, you are injuring yourself and that other person. You are giving your bread and getting stones in return. You are teaching and encouraging that person to give only stones. You are encouraging a life of selfishness and stupidity. You are preventing another sun from shining, another God or Goddess from maturing. You may likewise, through overmuch absorption of that person's inferior thought, be weighed down by it, crippled by it, and oppressed by an inertia or lack of energy not your own. You are swayed by their thought, and sometimes made to say and do things you would not were you freed from it. Your legitimate plans and schemes for your own

advancement are retarded or crippled because your
own thought, element of ambition, aspiration,
courage and energy are adulterated and alloyed
with the inferior thought of self-dependency which
is slavish. That mental slavery which is internally
content to depend entirely on another has always
in it the elements of cowardice and selfishness.

So if yours is the superior thought, and consequently you are the wiser person, you are in this
case the greater sinner and wrong-doer. Dependency is blind. It must be taught how to depend
on itself, and "work out its own salvation." Will
you then (who can see) allow the blind slave of dependency to travel on and on without ever calling
on its own rightful powers, without which it can
never gain permanent happiness?

The cultivation of self-independency and self-
reliance must commence in your own mind and by
yourself.

Have you your rights to assert before an unjust
person, or a reasonable request to make of him
which you may imagine he will consider as audaci-
ous? Is it a person of whose past injustice you can
speak freely before friends who sympathize with
you, but when before him, the one of all others who
should hear, you are silent? Why? Because you
are afraid to speak.

Deny in your mind at home, in the privacy of
your chamber, that you fear that person. See yourself in mind making to him a fair, calm and cool
statement of your case, and that without flurry
or loss of temper. Make this mental statement
in the sentiment and full desire of justice for both
of you. See yourself in what you call imagination,

as one who only wants what is right and nothing more.

When you do this you are actually doing your work. Your mind, your thought, as an unseen element travelling through the air, is at that very moment acting on that person's mind. As you have in mind presented your case in all justice and equity to him, so will your thought present itself as it flows from you to the person in question. You are then at that moment arguing your case with him and arguing with the element of thought, which is always the most powerful—the thought of justice, of good-will, which desires not revenge for wrong, but only redress.

But very many people who think of a wrong done them by another, think what they dare not say to that person face to face. They may think in the spirit of revenge, of "getting even," of causing some loss or suffering to the person in question because he has not done right. This process of thinking is the process of sending the thought element of some form of ugliness to the person thought of. It is the ugly thought of dependency—the slavish cowardly thought which puts out what it dare not put out in words before the person to whom such thought is sent. As so sent this thought element reaches the person in question. It irritates and annoys him. His thought of you is unpleasant. If in thought you see yourself as in fear of that person, so will he see, or rather feel you. This with a large class of mind, arouses contempt. That works against your case. If by yourself you place yourself in mind as one who is not afraid of him, yet is not revengeful—as one who, justice being done, is desirous afterward only of helping him, you are then sending him in thought the most powerful plea for yourself.

The "sense of justice" is not a mere metaphor. It is a quality in every person's nature as real as earth or air. In some it is more alive than in others. When you send out just calm, cool thought, it acts on that sense in another as light acts on your eye. It makes that person hear your just plea. He cannot avoid hearing it. When you place yourself in mind before yourself according to your highest ideal of manhood or womanhood, you are so placing your higher self before the person to whom you send your thought. If you so send yourself out in thought, you send out the strongest power.

The independent mind and life mean the freed mind. The freed mind is that which thinks no thought annoying to itself. It puts out then no element of thought save what is pleasing to it and others whom that thought reaches. The mind so originating and sending out such thought to others is ever building itself up on a basis of independence, of which the material (the thought of good-will) is gladly given it by others. When others so send their thought of good-will, they send also of whatever talent they possess. Your improvement in music, in painting, in any art or science will be quicker for the thought sent you by proficients in such art, who are friendly to you. Because as thought is element, the quality of their talent comes in their thought to you, is absorbed by you and is grafted on you so far as you have capacity to receive it. Your capacity to receive it depends on your freedom from all jarring of evil thought and your good-will and unselfishness. Selfishness will close you to the absorption of such thought. Unselfishness will open for you the doors to it.

It brings to you more life to think of things full of life and vigour and, so far as convenient, you should have such things in physical form before you. Such as children in bounding health, trees and flowers, birds and animals, not caged but in their native condition, water in motion, surfs, rapids and cataracts, moving clouds, and breezes. As either imaged or made in mind or sensed materially, the thoughts they suggest bring to you the current of live healthy thought, and this acts and enters into your body, building into it like material. Any verse or description of this character is a very healthy sentiment to dwell on, and if it recurs frequently to your memory it is a very healthy sign, for every time it does so recur it is bringing a literal solid and lasting good to mind and body.

Not only do these live healthy thoughts rest and clear the mind and strengthen the body, but the live strong thought-current with which you connect yourself thereby and which enters with them into your mind, sweeps away from it images of decay and death, cleanses it of unhealthy morbid imaginings, and as this clear, vigorous current gains more and more access to your mind, it will bear away wholly and for ever all the spiritual dust, cobwebs, vermin and uncleanliness which may have lodged there and caused you great pain.

As you grow more and more into this mental condition you will not only see but FEEL more and

more life in the many expressions of nature about
you.

Of whatever brings an emotion of fear or of rest
or pleasure there must be something, some element
to cause such emotion. The power we call spirit
expresses itself in many forms. It binds together
the tree in the shape we see it this month or this
year. It changes the shape of that tree and increases its girth and height next year. The same
mysterious force so forms and changes the shape of
bird and animal up to the period of maturity. It
is the moving power of the ocean of water below
and the ocean of air above.

We, with our physical senses, only see or feel the
physical part of the tree which spirit is so shaping.
Those physical organs do not sense the real, the
growing, moving power of the tree, bird, animal or
of ourselves.

But we have in embryo or latent, a set of senses
far finer and far more powerful which will when
ripened, sense, see and feel the real, the growing
power of the tree, and of all live growing things.
Those senses are already awakening and stirring
when we get pleasure in the thought of live, vigorous things above spoken of. They are then literally going forth absorbing the life or spirit of tree,
bird, animal, wave, wind, and flying cloud, and
bringing such life to us.

By this means or this mental condition, we may
get the life or growing power of the tree, bird, or
animal in ourselves. We get in the thought of the
billows, the surge, the cataract, the breeze, the gale,
their power in us. We may so get the youthful life
of plant, bird or animal. We want their life in its

youthful stage or up to maturity. That is their constructive period when they are building up their forms, or rather when this spiritual power is building up the material into such forms.

I do not mean that we should endeavour to force ourselves to the contemplation of these things. Forced contemplation is no contemplation at all. It is an attitude of mind having no power to absorb this life or spirit. It will only do harm. But if you are alive to the value of this kind of thought and desire it, it will come to you easily and naturally. You will then have more and more in your mind some image expressive of real vigorous life—the sun, a flower, a forest, an ocean beach, and such mind-images will in no wise interfere with the power and force of your thought in your business or art—any more than your occasional glance at the flower in your buttonhole, a reminder of the affection of your wife who placed it there, turns your thought from its proper course in the day's affairs.

This kind of thought awakens into life our now latent spiritual senses. The more these are so exercised and awakened, the more power have they. The more power they gain the more of this life can they bring from all these forms of material life, to repair, reconstruct and rejuvenate our bodies. For in reality it is mind or spirit that must be first so built, before the body can be. When the spirit is so attracting to itself healthy or constructive spiritual elements, these must in time assimilate and express themselves in the body.

Spirit is also at work on all decaying forms of material organization. It is simply taking them to pieces. It is as a tearing down of the house and out of its materials building a new. So the decomposed matter and its portion of spirit also enters into the composition of the new and growing plant to build that up.

But we do not want this power of spirit to act on us. We do not want to absorb the tearing to pieces or decaying power. Therefore, we will turn our minds from the destructive to the constructive spiritual forces, from the dead animal to the live one, from the weakness of material age to the force and fire of growing youth, from livid fungi in cellars and caverns to green, healthy growths in the sunlight, from stagnant pools to clear flowing brooks, from pictures of grief and gloom to pictures of joy, from sickness to health, from anxiety, seriousness and sullenness to cheer, liveliness and gaiety.

A lively strain of music brings to you the mind, sentiment or spirit of the person at the time of composing it. It brings also the spirit of those who are performing it. This is one great aid in bringing life. In the education of the future, music for every person will be deemed as necessary as are reading and writing at present, for it will be clearly seen that it is a most powerful means for bringing life, health and strength.

Many more persons have " music in them " than is generally imagined, and all of these can bring that music out of them on some instrument, or with the voice, even if unaided by others.

Music is inherent in every human spirit, and all spirit and some of our liveliest and most care dispelling melodies came without teachers, direct from the sunshine of the negro's heart while in captivity.

You do not need, in order to get and absorb their life or spirit, to be always in the material sight of trees, waters or the country. If it comes easy and convenient to be among these things—if you can step from your door in nature's heart or survey it from your window, so much the better. But to take long walks in field or forest for sake of exercise or for sake of the fresher element you suppose you may absorb in so doing is, in some cases, a means of injury. If the body is in any degree weak you may, in so doing, give out more strength than you receive and return weaker than before. If the body is relatively strong and the weather is harsh or bitterly cold, you may expend more strength in resisting the elements than you will gain. You are not then always placing your mind as a magnet to attract to itself the real force or element, of which all in forest and field is the outward or seen, covering. You may be among those seen coverings of tree, plant, animal and other things nearly all the time, and attract nothing of their force. If so much of your mind is expended in moving your body about, you may not keep it in the state to attract and receive of that spirit. This is the mental condition of many a farmer who at fifty is rheumatic, complaining and almost broken down. He may have lived amid the most beautiful scenery, but little of his mind was appreciative of it. Therefore he could not draw from it. He saw in the tree chiefly firewood, cut it down without a shade of regret, and valued nature chiefly as a marketable commodity. So in a measure is it right and necessary for him so to do to gain his subsistence under our present material system of life. But in seeing only in nature what he could turn into cash, and in feeling so little of its spiritual meaning, force and use, he cuts him self off from a source and supply of actual life.

But you, having a pleasure in the thought of these things, can draw their force or spirit to you in the city room, though the tall buildings about you almost shut out the sky, they cannot shut the forest, the breeze, the white-capped wave out of your mind. Nor can they prevent their spiritual force from coming to you and recuperating you in mind and body. For whatever you open your mind to, that it must attract.

Why do children so love to watch the falling snow-flakes? Because the spirit in its new body feels more intensely the spirit and force of the snow-flake. Because that spirit is then more alive and keen as to its spiritual sense than it will be a few years later when it is, as it were, crusted over and blunted as to such keenness by the duller thought and error absorbed of the older people with whom it is in daily contact. When the Christ of Judea said to the Jewish elders "Except ye become as this child ye cannot enter the Kingdom of Heaven," he meant as the text interprets itself to us, that with each new body used by a mind, there was in its earlier life a power of the spirit to sense and enjoy these forces, or the spirit in all things about it, and that the vigour and happiness of childhood came not, as is generally supposed, of the youth of the material body, but because the same spirit, having in the death of its last body cast off a load of erroneous thought it could no longer carry, in getting the new one, feels for a period its greater spiritual power.

This is precisely the mental condition we wish to bring to ourselves. We want also that spiritual force which the child does receive. That will keep us ever young. We want this power of childhood without its ignorance and helplessness. We want to be wise without being unattractive or decrepit. Greater wisdom must bring life and youth in every sense. Decrepitude and the decay of old age do not prove the highest wisdom. They do prove ignorance. "The tree is known by its fruit." A crop of weakness and failing powers proves defect somewhere.

Suppose that you should suddenly find you had some new organs and senses in you similar to your mouth, stomach, and sense of taste. Suppose also that in tree, plant, animal and all healthy and vigorous things, you should find a new substance or element unseen and unknown to you before, and that your new mouth was capable of taking it in and causing it to assimilate with and prove a source of strength and refreshment to mind and body.

Now, exactly in this relation do your other and spiritual senses serve you, and exactly so do they take in and assimilate these spiritual elements to refresh and build you up. Only these powers analogous to the material mouth, taste and stomach are now in a relatively weak condition. They are like the weak infant stomach and limited capacity for getting sustenance and strength from solid foods during its earlier years. But like the infants, these spiritual organs or capacities must grow stronger by exercise and get more from what they feed on as they grow stronger.

It is this healthy, vigorous thought, the spirit

essence and strength of nature and natural things that will not only benefit you, but will also unfold your latent talents, making of you greater and ever greater beings. There are no finalities in the empire of thought.

THE NECESSITY OF RICHES

IT is right and necessary that you should have the very best of all this world's goods—of clothing, food, house, surroundings, amusements, and all of which you are appreciative; and you should aspire to these things.

To aspire is not to covet another's possessions, or to desire to cheat another out of them. To live in squalor, to dress meanly, to eat coarse and inferior food, to live in barren and meanly-furnished rooms, or where the eye falls continually on dirt and degradation, is to cramp, starve, wound, and degrade the spirit. That will injure the body.

You really need all that your higher and most refined tastes call for and long for. You are the better for being surrounded by pictures and statuary of merit, by elegant household decoration, by the finest architecture. You are the better for having free access to the drama, for being able to travel and see other lands and peoples, and that in the best style and with the least inconvenience. You are the better for having your carriage and the means to entertain your friends, and thereby secure to yourself, under the best conditions, the best of association and social recreation. To have the cost of any comfort continually coming between you and the longing for its enjoyment, to see pleasures and long for them your whole life because you can-not afford them, to choke off hospitality when your heart is full of it, to be obliged to deny yourself of recreations and the needed rest they give mind and body, is to live a narrow, starved, cramped life. Starvation of taste, and starvation of any kind, is at the root of all excess and all degradation.

Your starved man overeats, and, having nothing better, will eat mouldy bread and tainted meat. Starved human tastes always denied healthy food create unhealthy appetites, and such starved tastes feast on the mouldy bread and tainted meat of the meretricious, low, cheap variety theatre, and all other places of similar character.

Refinement comes from the class having the most wealth, and, consequently, the most leisure. It is that class which best pays and encourages art. You do not get the elegancies of life from excessive toil and drudgery. You do find among that ele-ment the most coarseness, brutality, vulgarity, and degradation; and these things always accompany overworked bodies. That wealth is abused, that refinement may be mixed with effeminacy, is no proof against the great use and necessity for having, using, and enjoying wisely the best the soil can raise, and the best of all man's art and skill; or, in other words, the best of all we can do for each other; and in the coming Kingdom of Heaven, which is to be the kingdom of earth, that is what

men and women will be joyfully doing for each
other; but not without system, not without order,
not without the recognition and practice of the
law that a righteous and religious business consists
in such an interchange of commodities between
man and man, so that he who gives shall feel paid
by what he receives from another.

Is it not to our profit to have everything about
us as beautiful, as neat, as symmetrical as possible,
so that on whatever the eye falls or other sense
feels, only pleasure thereby shall be caused? For
every pleasant thought is a thing and a force, and
does you good. Is it, then, to the profit of mind
or body to have about you things repulsive, things
unclean, harsh, and angular in appearance, muddy
and smoky and gloomy, when every thought coming
from the sight of such surroundings is unpleasant?
And such force does really wound you and injure
you.

There is no merit in being poor or in desiring to
be poor. Poverty and a " hard time " in early life
do not develop and bring out qualities the sooner,
as so many argue. You might as well argue that a
plant starved of air, earth, water, and sunshine,
would the sooner become a healthy, fruitful plant.
Strong spirits, rich in thought, have risen above
poverty in spite of its impediments, and many a
strong spirit the world never heard of has been
crushed by it. The majority of the impelling
spirits and leading minds of the American Revolution—Washington, Jay, Adams, Hancock, Morris
—were relatively rich or prosperous, nor could
they have developed that mental or spiritual force
which really carried our cause to success, had the

Incessant physical drudgery of poverty been imposed on them.

Idea, and the best rounded-out idea, is born always of abundant leisure, and so are great achievements and great inventions.

Christ told his apostles to take neither purse nor scrip; but he did not tell them they should not have or enjoy all enjoyable things. By "purse and scrip," he implied the old and material methods for obtaining what they needed. He wished them to depend on spiritual law; that is, on their own spiritual or mental force, for bringing them the best things as they needed them.

Certain old proverbs encourage the idea that industry leads to wealth; but mere industry does not. Thousands are industrious, and poor all their lives. The point is, where and on what you put your industry. Industry, with little brains, saws wood and shovels coal for a living; industry, with more brains, buys a forest of wood, hires the sawyers and choppers, oversees industriously, and sells at a handsome profit. Neither does mere saving bring wealth. Thousands save and scrimp, and deny themselves luxuries and necessities, to lay up every spare penny, and are poor all their lives. They call it economy to walk a mile to save a cent car fare, and in so doing possibly expend enough force and strength which, rightly applied, would make ten dollars. They starve even their bodies, deny themselves nourishing food, live on the cheapest, and sleep in cold, damp rooms to save a dime, and in so doing contract disease and weakness. This is not real economy. It is worse than the wildest extravagance, for that may bring a

F

short pleasure. This course brings only pain, and only pain and loss are gained by it. Hundreds, if not thousands of this class, fall a prey to speculative schemers. Their carefully hoarded cash is invested in a mine which has next to no existence, save a name and a gilt-edged prospectus; or it vanishes in some wildcat stock, or in the construction of a railroad whose first shareholders never get a penny of their money back, or other glittering scheme promising large and certain returns, and performing only regular calls for more assessments, to save what is already put in.

Does " Early to bed and early to rise make men wealthy "? Who get up the earliest, work the most hours, and go to bed earliest? Thousands on thousands of the poor, going to their labours at dawn of a cold winter's morn, while the men who control the finances of the world rise at eight, breakfast at nine, get to business at ten, leave it at three or four in the afternoon, and recreate, possibly till midnight; nor would these men so control the domain of finance did they not give this ease and rest to the body (the spirit's instrument), in order to generate and use the force of that spirit.

So we find that the old worn-out maxims for attaining wealth do not " hold water." They are only true when taken with many modifications, and are but fragments of the real or spiritual law which brings abundance.

All material wealth is gained through following a certain spiritual law, or by the use, in a certain way, of human spiritual forces.

It is not a new law. It is followed in part, and quite unconsciously, and always has been, by those who gain wealth. But there is to be a fuller application of this law, whereby not only wealth will come to the individual, but at the same time health, and the ability to enjoy wealth. This law, used wisely and intelligently, is as much yours to profit by as it is the possession of any other person sufficiently clear in mind to recognize it.

Christ indicated to the apostles the spiritual law on which they should depend for all comforts, necessities and luxuries, when he said, "Seek ye first the kingdom of God, and all these things shall be added unto you." And in the kingdom of God, or the kingdom of spiritual law, the methods for obtaining all these things are essentially different, and almost the reverse of the purse and scrip, save and starve, body and mind abusing methods used by the kingdom of the material world to get money, and which, when so used, in the majority of cases, does *not* get it, or if it does, gets it at a terrible cost to the possessor.

You, now a spirit, using a physical body, are a part of God, or the Infinite Force of Good; and belonging to your spirit are powers, now possibly in embryo, but ever growing greater, as they have in the past and during vast periods of time, been growing to their present stature. To know and use these unseen forces intelligently, is to gain knowledge of and to use spiritual law intelligently, so as to bring you every possible good. Now, unconsciously, you may be using these very forces to bring you evil.

These forces are your daily, hourly thoughts. If you put those thoughts or forces in one direction, they will bring you health and the goods of this world to use and enjoy, but not to hoard; If you put them in another they will bring you disease and poverty.

Your every thought is a force, as real as a current of electricity is a force. The thoughts you are now putting out are now working to shape your face and body, affecting your health for good or ill, and making or losing for you money.

If you think poverty, you put out an actual force to attract poverty. If in mind you are always seeing yourself growing poorer and poorer, if at every venture you fear, and teach yourself to expect, to lose money, if your heart quakes every time you pull out your purse, you are by an inevitable force in nature, or spiritual law, attracting poverty. Your prevailing order of thought is a force which brings its like in physical things. If you live in a two dollar per week hall bedroom, and your thought every night and morning is, "Well, I suppose I must always live in this barren den," you are by such despondent state of mind creating in the invisible but most powerful element of thought, a power which will keep you in that room, and in a cheap, inferior corresponding order of life. If you say in your thought, and keep saying it, and keep so far as you can your mind in the state to say this: "I accept this room only as my temporary abode. I will have a better one, and after that a better one still, and everything else better," you are then, through the mysterious agency of your own thought power, bringing the better to you.

You have then set a magnet as real, though invisible, as the loadstone at work drawing the better to you, and you will find, as this state of mind is persisted in, that you will gradually drift away from cheap and relatively unsuccessful people into a more aspiring, broader, and successful order of mind.

When the hod-carrier thinks, aspires, plans, builds persistently in imagination something higher than carrying the hod, he is on the sure and only road to something better. Persistent desire or demand in thought for the better is the real force, impelling evolution from the lower to the higher. It is this that works, and has ever worked in all nature—in tree, animal, man, all forms of mind acting with physical and visible organizations—and it is this desire, this force, which in all forms of life has carried our planet from chaos to its present more improved and refined state. It was this desire, this almost unconscious prayer, that has, through countless ages, gradually changed the heavy, wallowing, unwieldy, and gigantic birds and beasts of a past far beyond human history, into the more agile, the more graceful forms of the animal life of the present (for we grant mind or spirit in greater or less degree to bird, animal, fish, reptile, and plant, and aspiration of spirit also) and it is this same aspiration or desire, the desire of the spirit in all forms of physical life, to be freed from the shackles and impediments of matter that shall, for the future, change plant, tree, and animal, into still finer and freer forms. It will transform men and women into beings and forces for illimitable and ever-increasing happiness, beauty and grandeur not now to be realized or imagined; for of all that is in the universe, and of all the possibilities in the universe, the present utmost scope of human imagination is but as the drop to the ocean.

Theology calls this desire prayer; and prayer is the great elevating force in the universe; and when you desire or demand anything, you pray for that thing, or, in other words, you set at work the force attaching that thing. You can so pray unconsciously for poor as well as for good things; and if you do, you attract poor things; and if in mind you see ever disaster, misfortune and the poorhouse, it is the same as praying for disaster, loss, and the poorhouse, and by this law, disaster, misfortune, and the poorhouse will come to you.

This force belongs to all of you. Such share as you have belongs to you and you alone. It has, through a part of vast periods of time, made you what you are. It is ever with you, increasing. You cannot stop that increase any more than you can stop this planet from improving and refining, for you and I are literal parts of this planet, and this planet is not a dead ball of earth. There is no death at all in nature. This planet is alive, all alive—a living, moving, growing, material expression of a gigantic spirit, even as your bodies are the visible expressions and instruments of your own invisible minds or spirits.

Christ was not poor in the things of this world. He could bring to him, and others, wine and food out of the elements through his power of thought, or spiritual power. He could save himself from shipwreck and drowning as no mere man of money could save himself. He could overcome the elements or create any material article he needed, through his power of concentrated thought.

That same power exists in embryo in every mind or spirit. It can be, and is to-day, exercised in dif-

ferent channels. It brings to those who exercise it,
though perhaps unconsciously, results in money
and possessions. It does not work so quickly as
with Christ. The results come more slowly; but
the power which brings millions to Jay Gould is a
spiritual power, a power working apart and often
far from his body, and a power, which, like fire or
electricity, unless used with the highest motive and
for the good of all, will *certainly*, in time, bring
great injury to those using it, either on this or the
unseen side of their lives.

In the following, lies one part of the spiritual law
for gaining what justly belongs to you.

It is a common reproach against ministers that
they "preach for pay," or preach for the largest
salary. A minister's calling is a business. He has,
or should have, as regards ideas, a valuable article
to give people. In the domain of justice, people
should compensate him in proportion to the value
of the article he gives. It is not justice in any business to expect or demand something for nothing,
or next to nothing.

If you hear a man every Sunday, and his thought
interests and strengthens you, and you go away
without contributing to that man's support, or desiring to, you are getting something and giving
nothing in return. But if you strongly and earnestly
desire to do something for that man, and cannot in
money, your thought is a power, and does him
good. If you give but a penny in such desire, that
penny is carrying to the preacher a thought force
for good, and is of far more value than thousands
given grudgingly. It was in this spirit that the
widow's mite, so commended by Christ, was given.

You enjoy and are benefited by that man's mind and talent as much as you are by a meal for which you are obliged to pay. You cannot get the gospel of good cookery without paying for it. No more should you get any other gospel. You would be ashamed to sit at a man's table every day, eating of the choicest food, without offering him something for it. You would be ashamed to see that man impoverishing himself and denying himself of comforts he needed while supplying you with that food. You would call him an unwise man for doing so. Exactly as unwise are they who think it their duty to preach or give of any gospel for nothing. Their sin is as great as that of those who take it for nothing. If you go into the streets and for the sake of pure benevolence give all your time and strength to people, you will become a pauper, both in mind and body.

The twelve apostles were not told to do this. They were told to depart from any house or any place where they were not properly received. They were told in case of such treatment, to shake from their feet the dust of such house or place as a "testimony against it." Lack of proper support is lack of being properly "received."

Some say: "Trust God in doing God's service." All manner of service rendered to humanity, such as religious, conscientious cooking, or house-building, or keeping a righteous store, is as much service in the spirit of infinite good as that of talking God's law to people; and trust in God is the following of God's law; and that is the law of justice and compensation; or, in other words, the law that *you cannot, without injury to yourself, do a service to another without in some way or shape receiving its value in return.*

If you do not, you will not only give yourself, your power, and all you have, away to others, but you may become a beggar, calling upon others to give you, without any return, that which in the injustice of ignorance you give, and even throw away, upon others who excite your sympathy; and in this way a man distinguished in the outside world for benevolence and a kind heart, may get from the woman, his wife, most of the strength he so freely distributes to others, and gives little or nothing back to her. For when a woman looks out, at home, for so many of the man's material comforts and necessities, and he depends on her, not only for the *entire* regulation of the household, his well-cooked breakfast, his punctually and properly sewed on shirt-buttons—if not to her care and foresight in paying the rent—even his moral support and moral backbone, drawn of her greater strength of character, or superior thought, and that man takes all this and expends it in the entertainment of other people, and comes to his home only a squeezed out, tired out, irritable sponge, to fill up and absorb more, and then leave her again to her own resources for social enjoyment, there is ignorant violation of the law of compensation, and the end and the penalty of such violation is a broken-down woman, and afterwards a broken-down man, who may never know that he was carried all his life by that woman, and that the strength he had was not his own but hers.

If the man's is the stronger thought, and the woman's the weaker, then he is the loser, and ultimately, so are both losers by the same process.

You will recollect that the force or thought you may have coming to you from another person is a current as real as a current of air or electricity, and that this force acts on you for good or ill. If that person's thought is richer than yours, that is, if such person has more foresight, is a better judge of character and motive, is more skilful to plan, and more determined, prompt and resolute to execute, that order of thought can feed your spirit, and give it strength,—and whatever strengthens the spirit strengthens the body,—and if yours is the inferior thought, and you cannot, in thinking of such person, send back a quality of element or thought of a corresponding value and richness, you are getting far more than you give. You are being fed of the richer element, and sending back the poorer. Yet, when so fed, you may be able to appropriate or absorb and use but a small part of what comes to you. The rest is wasted. If your thought is, in quality, equal to the other person's, you will give each other mutual strength. That is just compensation, and a righteous business transaction. These are agencies ever working all about us in the unseen kingdom of thought.

The sin and the penalty are as great for the one that gives such thought, without expecting or exacting a just return, as for the one who takes. It is this unconscious sin and the action of this little-known law that make poverty, and thousands on thousands of paupers and invalids, in every grade of society; and to-day many a rich man, whose force of thought, properly directed, would bring

money, revenues and possessions, expends the
same force on some person, on some one who gives
weakness back, and who wastes what is sent. That
same force or thought, more wisely directed, would
beget ideas, and ideas, when properly directed, can
always be turned into money; and the newest and
freshest idea is stronger than all the banks and
monopolies in the world.

Such as the discovery of petroleum, which was
an idea in some mind before discovery. Boring for
it was an idea in some mind long ere the boring.
Refining it was an idea long ere it was refined.
The invention of the modern elevator, thereby enabling buildings to be made higher, and so making real estate out of air space, was in idea long
before it was materialized in wood or iron; nor would
any of these ideas, all worth millions, have come
either to minds enfeebled by over-worked bodies,
or to minds which unconsciously allowed their
force to be drained from them in the way indicated
above.

" It is better to give than to receive," you quote.
It is better, in a sense. It is to the generous heart
more enjoyable to entertain a friend, to give a din-
ner, to relieve distress, than to be entertained, or
feasted, or relieved. But you find no precept of
Christ's against receiving. The very fact of giving
implies that some one must receive; but you must
take measures and use methods and foresight to
keep your reservoir filled up, so as to keep the
fountain of your benevolence playing. The sun
must draw moisture through evaporation from lake,
river, and ocean, before the clouds can drop that
moisture again to earth; and in the whole domain

of nature we shall find a well regulated and system
ized source and means of supply before there can
be giving out of that supply. That is business.

USE YOUR RICHES

FOR ages the idea has prevailed that to attain
the highest goodness, or the " kingdom of heaven," one must necessarily live poorly, while the
" wicked " live on the best.

On the contrary, in the future the best people,
those who through their ever-growing spiritual
power have " drawn nearer to God," or the Source
of Infinite Good, will through such power attract
to themselves and enjoy the very best of every
good thing.

When we live up to the fuller application of the
law, life will become a continual succession of
good things, to use and enjoy, but not to hoard ;
for it is a law working in all nature, through plant,
insect, animal, and man, that in order to have and
enjoy the new, we must first rid ourselves of the
old.

If the tree held stingily on to last year's fruit and
leaves, and refused to drop them, would not the
vents for next year's fruit and leaves be choked up?
If the bird, from dislike of parting with old possessions, could at its moulting season hold on to its
old plumage, would there come the newer and
fresher plumage? These are not far-fetched illus-

trations In evidence of the great spiritual law, that the old *must* be cast off ere the new can come; for in all of nature's workings, from the seed to the human soul, there is a wonderful and beautiful correspondence and analogy. The same law governs the growth and fruitage of a tree as of your spirit, only as regards your spirit it is infinitely more varied and complicated in its workings.

As with the tree and the bird, if you would the quicker enjoy the new clothes, the new house, the newer and better surroundings of every sort that you long for, cease in mind to cling and hang on to *all* things you have no use for in the present or immediate future. If you so hold on to half-worn trumpery of any sort, through the mere love of keeping, you are barring out the better thing coming to you. If you so hold on to the inferior, you keep from you the superior. If you will keep company with people who after all only tire you and bore you, who ridicule your ideas if you express them, and are utterly profitless to you, you keep the better people from you. If you cling to the old worn-out suit of clothes or seedy bonnet, and out of stinginess hate to give it away, and expend any amount of your force in haggling and dickering to sell it for a dime, you will not nearly as soon have the better clothing, for every thought put in the old represents just so much force, which could as well have been put on a plan to bring you hundreds of dollars instead of dimes.

It is the keeping of possessions, and the care of them, which you own and have used but which you cannot now use, which diverts your spiritual or thought power from gaining the fresher and better. It uses up that power on the care and keeping of things now of no use to you, and therefore a damage to you. You do not keep the top, the hoop, the clothing of your boyhood, and the valueless valuables with which you used to cram your pockets. Why? Because you know you have outgrown them, that they are now of no use to you; that you want your strength and time and thought for the acquisition of playthings more suited to the child whose body requires more yards of cloth to cover it.

If you have more things about you than you want for immediate use and enjoyment, they prove not only an annoyance, but that annoyance prevents you from gaining the newer and better. If out of desire of getting your money's worth you eat enough for three dinners in one, you make too large a contract for the stomach to fill, and defeat the purpose for which you put food in your body. If you have a horse in your stables you have no use for, it is more profitable to sell or give him away before he "eats his head off." If you have a garret full of old chests and chairs and furniture, or drawers full of half-worn clothing and shreds and rags and patches, all of which you keep simply from love of keeping them, or from the idea that you may need these things some time or other, it is far more profitable to sell them or give them away. Because these old and unused things do keep newer and better things from you, by being a care, a load on your mind.

Thousands of people go through life lugging and blacking themselves with old pots, pans, and kettles they have no use for. What would you

think of a man, who, for sake of keeping a crowbar, should chain it to his ankle and drag it along
with him? You can so chain crowbars to your
mind. Many a house owned and hired to others
proves a crowbar to its owner. Taxes and repairs
eat up the rent, and the force put out through the
care and anxiety it causes, represents just so much
capital stock, which, if properly expended, would
bring in far more money.

One secret of the kings of finance is that they
know when to rid themselves of possessions on
seeing how those possessions can be of no farther
use to them. In so doing they work by a spiritual
method. Far-sighted men are at this moment "un-
loading" themselves of properties which they see
have no immediate money in them, and near-
sighted men are at this moment buying those properties, which will for years lie on their hands a
care without recompense, and an incumbrance and
obstacle to more immediate gain. The real cost of
keeping things is the amount of thought you put in
their keeping. If you will keep an old bedstead or
bureau, or anything else you never have any use
for, and carry it about with you at every house-
moving, and put study and calculation as to the
place it shall occupy, and worry then because it
takes room which you need for every-day purposes,
you are putting from time to time force enough on
a (to you) useless article which, if properly directed,
would buy a hundred new bureaus. In this way
does this, the blind desire of mere keeping and
hoarding, keep many people poor, and even makes
paupers.

Mere hoarding is not business. If every one put

away money as they gained it, and lived on as little as possible, and continually decreased their expenses, the world's business would soon stop, not so much from lack of money lying useless in chests and old stockings, but because there would soon be little left for people to do to gain money. It is large outlays, expensive and luxurious styles of living, the making of the costliest articles, the erection of magnificent buildings, and not hovels, the demand for the very best of everything, that keeps the labourer, the mechanic, the artist in any department, at work, and keeps the stream of wages pouring into their pockets.

Mere hoarding brings nothing in the end to him who hoards but pain and trouble.

The miser is but a one-sided success. He has gained money only to pile it away in vaults. That money brings him only the gratification of owning it and of adding to the pile. That is but a mania. He gets from his money little pleasure for his body, little pleasure coming from the gratification of intellectual or artistic tastes. He owns only a pile of stamped metal or paper, substantially lives in a poor house, and is a poor man.

Families doing no business, and living entirely on the interest derived from hoarded wealth gained by their ancestors, last but a few generations. They die out, because their spiritual activities and forces become inert and sluggish, from lack of exercise. They live the lives of drones, and as one generation succeeds another their minds grow feebler. They become unable even to hold their possessions against the rising and more active forces about them.

In point of wealth, where are the families that existed in this country a century ago? In most cases out of sight, impoverished and superseded by those now so prominent in the world of business and finance—the new men, poor materially at the start, but having minds richer in force. They have exercised that force and achieved their partial successes, and their grandchildren or great grandchildren may become paupers, if content merely to exist on incomes, and give no play to their forces. Even in England it becomes difficult to keep wealth in families as handed down by entail from father to eldest son, for even when sons are supplied they often prove unable to keep the property left them, and even the bequeathed title and possessions of a duke or earl may not prevent that duke and earl from being very low in the scale of intellect.

But the life using this present body, is the merest fragment of our real existence. There is an inevitable penalty to be surely paid by the hoarder of money or other possessions, on losing his body. He has not "passed away," he has only passed from physical sight. He has the same desire as ever to control his property and handle his money. He cannot lift a farthing of it in material substance. But he knows that the money he once called his own exists, and where it is. He knows as well as ever the people still having material bodies he once dealt with, while he to them is a blank—nothing. Though he may have "willed" his millions to others, he cannot will the desire for their possession out of his mind. If such desire for mere keeping without using existed during the

G

life of the body, it will be just as strong after the
death of the body. Your mental characteristics,
your temper, your inclinations, your passions, your
appetites, are no more changed immediately on the
death of your body than they are changed to-day,
when you cut off a part of that body, say an arm or
a leg.

If at the death of your body you are a mere
hoarder of things, you will be tied to those things
by bonds or chains, which, though invisible, are as
real as chains of iron. If, during the body's life
your thought is put entirely on the gold or bank-
bills in the safe or vault, if nine-tenths of your time
is occupied in planning to add to that hoarded and
useless store, you are making in the element of
thought, chains or filaments tying you to the gold,
or bills, or house, or lands once yours and now
controlled by others, and yours will be the pain of
seeing all these things used as others please, while
you can neither get away from nor cease to claim
them as your own.

It is this law of being and of attraction that has
forced people, after losing their bodies, to remain
long periods of time at or near places where, when
in visible form, they buried treasures, or in houses
they formerly owned or occupied, which they do
literally " haunt " and are sometimes seen by a
physical eye, temporarily clairvoyant, or through
the disembodied person's being able to act for a
time through or by some physical agency.

" Ghost stories," so called, have prevailed in
every age, in every nation, among people widely
separated from each other, and have been told
ever since human history was given, either in writ-

ing or tradition. They are based on truth and reality.

You do not "pass away" from earth at all on losing your body, nor do you "come back" in the sense of coming from some far-off place. You are here still, though unseen, among your friends, if you have any, at your desk, your store, your workshop, where, possibly a few hours previously, your body dropped lifeless, because your spirit had no longer strength to carry it; and if while using the body your heart, soul, and mind were ever bent, wrapped up and directed only to that one place or occupation, and you had little or no interest in anything else—to no art, to the bringing out of no other talent within you save that of mere money getting and property hoarding, then to that one place will you be bound by these invisible ties, nor can you break them and get elsewhere until you learn to cultivate your other powers; in other words, to throw the current of your thought on other interests and pursuits. In so doing you create a literal magnet of thought element as you centre yourself more and more in such pursuit; and as this, aided by your earnest desire, grows stronger and stronger, it will attract you more and more from the old centre or place to which you are tied, and at last break such tie altogether.

If you do not cultivate your other and latent resources, yours will be the misery of being so bound to that house, place, or pursuit, though it be carried on in a manner against your inclination, though old acquaintances drop out and strangers take their places, though your family mansion passes into unknown hands,—and to-day many a person with-

out a visible organization lingers in misery in and
about the house he once owned, tied to it, because
he can centre no interest in anything else, a
stranger in the place he tries to call home; and if
he approach his own fireside it is only to be repelled
or annoyed by the thought atmosphere of the new
people about it.

"It is easier for a camel to pass through the
needle's eye than for a rich man to enter the kingdom of heaven," one may quote against us. The
" kingdom of heaven " is located in no particular
place in space, and can be and will be wherever
mind grows wise enough and strong enough to
make it, be it on the earth stratum of life or elsewhere. The "rich man" who cannot enter is really
the poor man who loads himself down with things
he cannot use or allow others to use,—a human
dog in the manger, spending all his force in stand-
ing guard and snarling over what he cannot use and
will not allow others to use, and is at last killed by
the continual generation within himself of the
poisonous thought of snarling and covetousness.
But the rich mind and the rich man, who, knowing
the law, has the secret and power of attracting the
world's best of everything to him, not only that he
himself may use and enjoy, but contribute to the
good and happiness of all, lives, in so doing, in the
kingdom of heaven. He becomes, as his power
and wisdom increases, as a growing river, an ever-
flowing stream, ever bearing from the mountain
tops both water and soil to fertilize the plains; but
if the river hoarded soil and water, what would be
the result?

Neither " moth and rust nor thieves " can affect

possessions which are used but not hoarded. The plant appropriates and uses only what it needs for the hour, of air, water, sunshine, and earth element. If more is supplied to the plant than is necessary for its present needs, blight and disease are the result. When man, through his artificial and unnatural methods of cultivation, over-stimulates vegetable growth by excess of fertilizing material, an insect life is bred of the plant. That insect is destructive to that plant, because there has been an over-supply and a hoarding of some element in undue quantity. Element in any form of life must be used, not hoarded, if real profit and pleasure is desired from it. Moths on plants and moths and rust in anything are themselves provisions and methods from the Source of Infinite Good to prevent hoarding. Neither moth nor rust really destroys. They take elements to pieces, useless in their present form, and scatter and distribute them, that they may enter into new forms of combination and serve new uses.

If you owned this whole earth, in the worldly sense, you could only use and enjoy such portion of its air, sunshine, water, foods, and forces, as would satisfy your needs for the hour and the day. The keeping of the rest would ultimately destroy your body. Your ownership would be a farce. You have no control over the planet's revolutions, over the tides, the seasons, or the river's flow to the seas. You have no power over earthquake or storm. You cannot keep your body on the land you think you own, when the time comes that your over-burdened spirit loses the power to hold itself to that body. You lose your body, and what then?

You are a miserable prisoner, tied to numberless tracts of land, houses, and all other physical properties, unable to control them, to use them, to enjoy them, and worse still, to free yourself from the delusion that still you do own them. You are really insane. You have then " gained the whole world and lost your own soul." That is, you have not yet found your soul; or, in other words, the power latent in you ever to increase your thought force so as to draw all things to you, to use and enjoy and then rid yourself of, so as to gain the newer and better.

But following the law common to all life, that of throwing off the old in order to receive the new, exactly as your body throws off what it cannot assimilate and convert into bone, muscle, and blood, will give your spirit more and more power. You are then going forward on the road to complete command over all material things. You will then eventually have power to heal your body of any ailment, to make it ever more perfect, strong and healthy, to be at last beyond the reach of all disease, and as a consummation, to be able to put on or take off that body as you would a garment. So freed from it, your real self is independent of all ordinary means of locomotion. You visit other lands and while there make a body for transient use. These things have been done in past ages. They have been realized in later days to an extent among certain Oriental races. They are certain possibilities for the future.

The basis for attracting the best of all the world can give to you, is to first surround, own, and live in these things in mind, or what is falsely called

Imagination. All so-called imaginings are realities and forces of unseen element. Live in mind in a palace, and gradually palatial surroundings will gravitate to you. But living thus is *not* pining, or longing, or complainingly wishing. It *is* when you are " down in the world," calmly and persistently seeing yourself as up. It is when you are now compelled to eat from a tin plate, regarding that tin plate as only the certain step to one of silver. It is *not* envying and growling at other people who have silver plate. That growling is just so much capital stock taken from the bank account of mental force.

But when you have no present use for your palace, give others the use of it, or it will become your poorhouse. If you store it away, you store with it so much weight on your mind, so much thought to be expended in storage, so much spiritual force which might otherwise have been put in the cultivation of a talent. If you have five talents or ten talents it is your necessity to cultivate them all at times, and you want for such cultivation all your power unshackled. You are an institution, and if you do not cultivate every department of that institution, every taste and power you feel within you, you will suffer. The whole man is merchant, mechanic, physician, actor, painter, sculptor, all and everything longed for by his ambition and inspiration. Eternity has time enough for all these, as recreations. You cannot reduce such a man to beggary. Beggary is not in him. Destroy every material thing to-day he possesses, and to-morrow his force will be attracting more. Men are living to-day who *partly* illustrate this law. Others are to come who are to make the illustration far more perfect, and live lives which will fill the world with wonder and admiration.

THE USES OF SICKNESS

IN this era of our planet's existence, there can scarcely be for anyone entire escape from ills of the body. But there are two entirely different methods of treating in mind those states of the body we call sickness. The right one is to consider and hold in mind, and ever desire earnestly, that you may be led into more and more faith that all pain, sickness, and debility, of whatever nature, are but efforts of the spirit to purge itself, and throw off from the body that which has become too gross for your spirit to use.

Here bear in mind the fact which it is necessary often to repeat, that your spirit is one thing and your body quite another; that your spirit is an ever-increasing power, the growth of ages, and that your body is only its temporary instrument, for use in this one present phase of existence.

We are ever liable to glide unconsciously into the old belief in which we have been educated, that all there is of us is the physical body. Without the spirit, the body is only the engine, without steam to move it.

An ever-increasing realization that spirit and body are two distinct things, and that the spirit is the only moving, building, and working force for the body, will prove a great help to your spirit to act favourably on the body, and reconstruct it anew.

The second wrongful and injurious method of using sickness, is to hold and firmly believe that you are nothing but the body you use; that it is only the body which is sick; that its only cure lies in material remedies; that its present state of sickness or debility is but an unmitigated evil, and not the means whereby it is being freed from a load of relatively dead matter, too lifeless and inert for the spirit to use. This indicates utter ignorance of the spirit; and such ignorance of the spirit brings on more and more of disease and corporeal deadness, until at last your real and only power, your spirit, is unable to carry the half dead body any longer. It frees itself from such encumbrance. You call that death. It is only the dropping of a load by the spirit, too heavy longer to be carried.

There are in the world to-day many people who are already half dead. In other words, their spirits do but half carry their bodies. The stooping shoulders, bent knees, feeble gait, and general failing senses of a man or woman at the age of sixty, are so many evidences that the mind using that body is in utter ignorance of its power to recuperate and regenerate that body. All that power through its character of belief, is now being used to destroy the body. If the mind is in the right belief, the body will come out of its trial purified of grossness, more refined, more active and stronger than ever. In the physical sense, it has grown younger instead of older.

Even if you can but entertain and give this idea

a respectful hearing, It will make a great difference for the better in your physical state. Because, in even changing to this extent the attitude of your mind, you have opened a door for your higher self to work for good upon the body. Belief in the truth will then help the mind to more command over the body. Command of mind over body must ultimately free the body from every ill and pain. The physical trials you may now pass through are not always to be necessary in the purging and refining process. These first trials are the hardest. As the spirit gains more and more supremacy and faith in these truths, which will be more and more proven, the body will pass through the changes incident to the growing power of the spirit with less and less pain and inconvenience.

If you receive a new and truthful idea, it will work a change in the body. Your present muscle, blood and bone are all material expressions of, and physical correspondences of, your prevailing order of thought. Change that thought, and a change must take place in the character and quality of the seen material forming the body. If the unseen power of the body is changed, that which is seen must change.

Such changes, to a limited extent, are constantly at work in daily life. Give a person in despair or discouragement, hope, or promise of something better, and a change in the body is soon manifest. The eye grows brighter, the muscles are braced more firmly,- and every movement shows more vigour. A new element of thought is not only act ing on that body, but has actually entered into and assimilated with it.

On the contrary, throw a thought of terror suddenly into the mind, and such is the effect of that thought-element acting on the body and actually entering into the composition of the body, that, as known in varying instances, faces grow pale, knees totter, weakness succeeds strength, digestion is checked, insensibility is sometimes brought on, the hair has bleached in a few hours, and even instant death has been thereby caused.

The terrifying cry of "Fire!" in a crowded theatre, the cry of alarm raised in a crowd of people, bring an element and a force to act first on the minds, and next on the bodies of those people, which, though unseen, are as real, in a material sense, as any noxious gas or vapour, such as the fumes of burning charcoal, which, though unseen, prove their existence by their fatal results.

All pain comes of the effort of the spirit to force new life into a part of the body lacking life. Or it comes of the spirit's effort to throw off altogether such part lacking life, and replace it with new material. In cases when the spirit ceases from such effort, there comes cessation from pain and insensibility, the forerunner of the body's death.

When disease is regarded in what we will here call the remedial light, life assumes an entirely new aspect. The life of the body becomes then a succession of rebirths or changes from coarser to finer material, each birth or change being less painful than the one preceding, until, at last, such change is accompanied only by a period of languor and physical inactivity. Or, in other words, the spirit is making the body into its own image, so that it shall be the perfect instrument to carry out its desires. Then body and spirit are wedded. They are as one.

If the mind or spirit in ignorance accepts implicitly these old errors, then that mind is already sick, though the body it uses is strong. If the mind is sick, the body in time must become sick. But when the awakened mind refuses any longer to accept these old errors, and desires that it may come to know and reject all other error, of which it may now be unconscious, that mind is relatively healthy. It is then on the road to higher and higher health. True, its body may for periods be prostrated through the changes, which a change from lower to higher mental conditions will bring about. But such periods of physical ailment become as ends to a higher health, because the mind, being in the right direction, is pushing the body in that direction, whereas the mind in ignorance, not having the vestige of an idea that it is the power which rules the body, accepts blindly the error which the body in a sense teaches it, and then uses all its force to build on and increase that error. The body used and ruled by such a mind will have disease in its worst form, until such body is at last destroyed. The body used and ruled by the mind inclined in the right direction may have ailment and suffer, but it will, if the faith of its spirit has grown strong enough, come out of the trial purified, refined, strengthened, and having more power than ever to resist evil and prevent the absorption from lower minds of their lower and injurious thought, which to the sensitive person is a prolific source of disease.

In many cases, through natural birth, the spirit is given a body with which it is at total variance.

That body may come into the world freighted with a certain mind of its own. That mind comes of the lower and erroneous thought absorbed in gestation, infancy, and youth. That lower mind may rule the body for years, or for its whole physical lifetime. The real self, the real spirit, may only influence what may be called a fragment of that body, and this only at certain periods favourable to its access. The lower mind may rule much of the time with low and gross desires. For the whole thought-current of the lower or "carnal mind" rules on this stratum of life, and meets the higher mind with obstacles or temptation at every point.

For such a spirit even to preserve at all its present body, may involve much pain and sickness. This comes of the war betwixt spirit and body. The spirit seeks to fashion the body in accord with itself, and tries to throw off the old dead thought in which the body has been educated. The body resists. The body has an individuality of its own. It desires to preserve that individuality. It feels in the effort of the spirit not only an invasion of such individuality, but an attempt to destroy that individuality for ever. This is actually the case. If the individuality of the body is one of error and belief in untruth, it cannot last. It must be destroyed. Nothing can endure permanently but what is based in truth. Sickness, then, is a means for the removal of the old body, exactly as when you make a new wall of an old one, by taking away, piecemeal, portions of the old, replacing them with new and sound material, until the wall is altogether new.

There may be nothing new under the sun, but there are things innumerable, now unknown, which would be new to us. We have touched hardly the edge of our real life, and know little what it means really to live.

Nor can we take in at once much of what is new without danger. Truth must be received in small doses, otherwise a sudden flood of light, a sudden revelation of life's possibilities, would cause so sudden a physical change, and so great a disturbance betwixt spirit and body, as possibly to destroy the body. The removal of the old, and its replacement by the new, should be a gradual process. It is akin to digestion. Too much food taken at once into the stomach brings pain and disturbance. Too much of new idea taken at once, is the putting of new wine into old bottles. The old bottle represents the old body, the new wine is new thought. All idea is actual force; and if more force be received than the old body can appropriate, there is a possibility that its working will burst the bottle.

The new material given you by this change is new and true thought or idea. That will materialize blood, bone, muscle, and nerve into a newer, finer, and stronger quality of seen substance.

A child bred in the belief that its real self is only the body it uses, that there is no power behind that body, which, if known and rightly directed, can ever rehabilitate it with new element, recuperate it, and ever make its material substance over and over again, each time newer, finer, and stronger, such a child—and many such there now are—not only has within it what may be termed the "seeds of disease," but through its total ignorance, combined with the ignorance of other minds about it, nearly all the power of its spirit is worked the wrong way

—worked to feed and strengthen disease, and so, at last, make the body unbearable for the spirit.

There is a kind and quality of mind affecting us all more or less. It is sometimes called the "unconscious mind." It is belief in error, absorbed from others possibly in infancy and youth, which we have never questioned and never doubted— never thought to question or doubt, and which we blindly go on believing, scarcely knowing it is our belief. But such belief affects us for good or ill, just as much as that of which we are conscious of believing.

Holding such unconscious error to-day, thousands of hearty, athletic young men, now in the fullest possession of vigour and muscular strength, believe that at the age of fifty this vigour must begin to lessen, and that between sixty or seventy, some "ill that flesh is heir to" must necessarily beset them, and ultimately carry them off. To say to them, seriously, that a time is coming when man's superior knowledge will enable him to keep his body as long as he pleases, and in an ever-improving condition, would immediately call from them either ridicule or that obstinate incredulity which will not for one moment entertain a new idea as a possibility.

Nothing is more dangerous than that permanent state of mind which instantly rejects and refuses for one moment to entertain, hospitably, a new idea, because it seems to that mind wild, unreasonable, and visionary. It is the same condition which in years gone by scornfully rejected steam and electricity as "new-fangled notions." It is the condition which makes for itself a rut of thought and occupation, and travels round and round in it without any advance forward to newer life and possibilities. It is the condition leading surely to fossilization of both mind and body.

Thousands are to-day unconsciously imprisoned in the idea that what all human or physical life has been in the past, that it must necessarily be in the future, and that it must necessarily involve the three periods of youth, maturity, and decay. To believe this so implicitly, makes these phases of life inevitable for the believer, and bars the door against any new possibilities.

Flesh is heir to no ills save those bequeathed the flesh by the spirit in ignorance. The spirit once in the truth can bequeath the flesh only more and more life; in brief, "life everlasting."

Do you ask what are some of the errors unconsciously held by thousands about us? An individual whom you know to be a demagogue or charlatan, passes with thousands as a great man. A system of education which you know to be honey-combed with falsity and the blind repetition of custom, they accept as perfect. War between nations which you know to be but blind idiocy, they accept as a "political necessity," because from infancy the sound of those two words has been trumpeted into their ears and remains clinched there. Customs, usages, and habits, which you know to be not only useless, but resulting in injury or inconvenience, are perpetuated from generation to generation, unthought of, unquestioned.

The cruelty wantonly inflicted by our race on beast and bird in their natural state, in slaughtering and mutilating them for mere amusement, as well as the imprisonment of every species of biped and quadruped, dooming the inhabitants of field, forest, and air to an unnatural and suffering life, simply that we may stare at them behind their bars, is another evidence of the unconsciousness of our race to the wrong and injustice which it permits, and even endorses as right and proper.

The degraded estimation in which woman is held by great masses of men; the degraded estimation which she accepts without question or protest herself; the estimate of her by so many men, either as a pleasing toy or a convenience; the ignorance and denial by most men that she is equal to him in power for business or any pursuit, as well as the ignorance and consequent denial, both on his or her part, that she is, when rightly understood, a necessary factor to his highest success,—all these are still unconscious errors leading to grievous ills in the minds of millions on millions.

The still prevailing ignorance that thought is an element and force, working results miles from the body it uses; that every thought or idea of ours is like an unseen magnet, which, if held to, will bring to us in material things the likeness of that thought; the common idea that it matters little what we think, so long as our thought is not known; the ignorance that what we think of others and ourselves has everything to do with our health and fortunes, for happiness or misery; the sloughs of physical misery and mental disturbance, into which so many plunge themselves unconsciously, through association with minds lower than theirs, and so absorbing and living in such lower thought; the ignorance that every individual has lived in the past other lives, and must in the future live more,

H

either with or without a body,—all these form but a fragment of the unconscious errors prevalent all about us. For the mind ever calling for more truth and light, every bodily trial results in a greater and greater awakening to these and hundreds of other errors, which, so long as held in mind, bring inevitably results in pain and misery to us.

"The truth shall make you free," says the biblical record. It is so. The truth shall free us from every form of physical and mental suffering; and when the God in yourself rules completely the old and lower self, all tears are then wiped from our eyes.

THE DOCTOR WITHIN

"FAITH is the *substance* of things hoped for." If you keep in your mind an image, or imagination, of yourself in perfect health, and full of strength and activity, you keep the forces working to make you so. You are constructing out of the unseen substance of thought a spiritual self (the healthy self hoped for); and this spiritual self will in time rule the material body, and make it like unto itself. If your stomach is weak, refuse in imagination to see it a weak stomach: see it only a strong stomach. If your lungs are weak, see in your mind's eye your lungs are strong. If your body is weak and sluggish, see yourself in imagination as you were when a boy or girl, when your limbs were full of activity, and you took delight in

scrambling over fences and climbing trees. You
are then putting out the "substance" of the thing
or condition of body "hoped for." As you continue to see yourself thus, the gradual change in
your physical condition for the better will increase
your faith that this law is a truth. Keep to this
thought of yourself as strong, active, and vigorous,
week after week, month after month, year after
year, and you fix more firmly in mind yourself as
free from all disease. It will be a confirmed habit,
or, as we say, "second nature," for you so to imagine yourself.

What you think or hold most in mind or imagination, that you have most faith in. If you imagine
a bugbear, much of the time you will make a reality
of such imagining. The "confirmed invalid" sees
himself in his "mind's eye" only as sick. He puts
out, or imagines, the wrong image, or imagination. He is unconsciously working the same law.
The invalid who always sees himself as sick, is in
reality constructing a sick body. You can make a
weak stomach for yourself by always in imagination seeing your stomach as weak. The great
trouble and error of to-day is, that, so soon as any
organ is a little overtaxed or strained, its possessor
is apt to think of it only as weakened and diseased,
and in thought dwells only on such weakness: in
this, unfortunately, he is too often assisted by others.
As all thought put out is substance, the result is,
there is by such means made for him, first, spiritually, a stomach, or lungs, or kidneys, or other organ,
more imperfect; and this imperfection is embodied
and expressed in the material lungs, stomach, kidneys, or other organ.

It cannot be told too often, that all material things are the outgrowth or product of spiritual or unseen forces. Whatever you think of is *made at once* in unseen substance. As soon as made, it commences at once to attract its like order of substance to itself: so, no matter how weak you are, when in mind you see your body active, strong, and vigorous, you have really made the spiritual body so. That spiritual body is drawing, then, the elements of health and strength to itself. Always in mind see yourself well when your body is sick. This is a simple process, but it involves a wonderful and wonder-working law. When in mind you see yourself diseased, though your body may be so, you are working this law the wrong way.

The imagining of a fresh, sound, vigorous body, is in actual substance, though unseen, a fresh, sound, healthy, and vigorous body. It is a spiritual reality. The material body must grow to be like the spiritual reality. If your body is weak, do not see it in your mind's eye as weak. See yourself full of life and playful vigour. Don't see yourself as an invalid propped up in a chair, or confined to the house, though for the time being your body is in such conditions. You are healing yourself when you see yourself running foot-races. You are keeping yourself an invalid when you see yourself ever as one. Don't expect or fear sickness or pain for to-morrow, no matter what sickness or pain you have to-day. Expect nothing but health and strength. In other words, let health, strength, and vigour be your day-dream. The desirable condition of mind is better expressed by the word " dream " than by the terms " hoping " or " expecting."

" Dreamers " do far more than the world realizes. The " day-dream " of a person who may sit for an hour almost unconscious of what is going on directly around him, is a force working out results in the unseen and mighty kingdom of thought, concerning which we know so little. But at present, he whose thought is so disengaged from the body as to make him for the time quite unconscious of its existence, having no knowledge of the power he is using, no belief that it is doing something, has consequently no faith in it; and without faith, most of the result must be lost.

If you know nothing of gold-mining, or of the formations in which gold is found, or of the methods for extracting it from the soil, you may dig in rich gold-bearing earth for months, and cart if off to fill in sunken lots. With no knowledge of the treasure in your soil, you have no faith in it. We are, as regards our mental or spiritual powers, in an analogous condition. Yet every imagining is an unseen reality; and the longer and more firmly it is held to, the more of a reality does it make itself in things which can be seen, felt, and touched by the physical senses. Dream, then, as much as you can by day of health and vigour. The more you so dream of it by day, the more likely is your thought to enter the same vigorous domain at night, and so recuperate you all the quicker. But if you dream by day of sickness or weakness, your thought at night will be the more apt to connect itself with the current of sick, weak, diseased thought, and you are, on waking, the worse for it. Ignorantly you may store gunpowder in your cellar, thinking it some harmless material. A spark may then

destroy your house and your body. In an analogous manner menkind are now constantly bringing
pain and evil on themselves through an unwise or
ignorant use of their mental forces. As we think,
imagine, or dream, so can we store up gold or
gunpowder. A day-dream, or reverie, is an outflow of force working results. The more abstracted
the reverie, the greater is the force working separate and apart from the instrument, the body.
When for a time you can forget, or lose consciousness of, your physical self and immediate surroundings, you are working your spiritual or thought
power possibly a hundred or a thousand miles away.
All occult power, so called, all the miracle power
of biblical record, was wrought by this method. If
thought can be concentrated in sufficient volume
on an image in mind, it can produce instantly
that image in visible substance. This is the only
secret of magic. Magic implies the instantaneous
production of the visible by such concentration.

The power of Christ's thought concentrated on
an imagining, or mental picture, could produce
that imagining in visible substance, as it did the
loaves and fishes. All minds have these powers
and possibilities in embryo.

Faith is indeed as the "grain of mustard-seed"
to which, as to growth, it is compared in the New
Testament. But it can grow for evil as well as
good, and if for evil, may become a tree in which
every foul bird of evil omen will come and build
its nest. Your evil or gloomy imagining is faith in
that evil. Your fear of a disease is faith in the
perpetuity and increase of such disease. You have
a slight derangement of stomach or kidney or

other organ. So, having it for one day or a few days, you begin to expect it. You think of it only as an unhealthy organ. You never in mind see it as a sound organ. You may be then told it is in a dangerous condition. You have a name possibly given to the ailment which is suggestive of great suffering, debility, and ultimate death. All this is help to faith in evil. The force of other minds may be added to yours which increases that faith. Friends and relatives may be anxious on your account, and fearful, and continually reminding you how careful you should be. Every thing tends to make you see yourself sick, weak, and enfeebled. You have not in your own mind an imagining of the part affected as sound or healthy. None send you their thought, or imagining, as vigorous and healthy. The spiritual thought-constructions sent you are all in the opposite direction. The spiritual force sent you is really all for evil. If your friend says he "hopes you may get well," he says it with an accent and expression which says he fears you may not. And so your faith in an evil is constantly increased. You always get the "substance" of the thing feared or expected as well as hoped for. In this case you get the substance of evil. You get more disease, more weakness by the same law, or force, which can, otherwise directed, bring you health. You are taught to have more faith, or belief, in sickness than in health. "According to thy faith," says the biblical record, "shall it be given thee"; and accordingly you have given you sickness, because you have most faith in sickness.

Nature never really grows old as we understand that term. She is ever casting off her worn-out

physical envelopes, or forms of expression. We say
the tree decays. But do we not see the new tree
springing from the rotten stump of the old one?
That is the same tree. In other words, it is the
spirit, or force, of the tree we called old, material-
izing a new form of expression. That process has
been going on through countless ages. That species
of tree was far coarser than now in some far-off
past. It has, through its successive regrowths,
been growing finer and finer, and is to grow finer
still.

In all animal and other organized life, we find
periods of repair and recuperation preparatory to a
certain newness of life, and renewal of organization, as when the crab or lobster casts its shell, the
snake its skin, the bird in its moulting-season casting its old plumage, the animal shedding its fur. In
all these organizations other changes go on, which
we do not see. During these periods, the bird,
animal, and fish are weak and inactive. Nature
demands rest during this reconstruction. Such reconstruction is going on internally in the organization as well as without.

All natural law, as seen in the lower forms of
organization, extends to the higher. This same law
extends to mankind. There come temporary periods
in every person's life, when all the activities, forces,
organs, and functions are more sluggish. We are
then undergoing our moulting process. Nature is
laying us up for repairs. If we obeyed her demands,
we should come forth in a few weeks or months
with a renewed life and a renewed body. All that
Nature asks of us, is that we give mind and body
the rest they call for while in the repair-shop.

We speak of people of " middle age " as having reached their greatest amount of power and activity. After this period, it is inferred as the " law of Nature," that we decline gradually into " the sere and yellow leaf." This faith in "old age" and weakness, by the same spiritual law makes old age and weakness.

The "turn" at middle age, or a little after, means that the physical body you have been using is giving birth to a new one; in other words, the old is being re-formed, and giving place to the new. During such process of re-formation, a great deal of rest is required. Your real, invisible, spiritual self is busy at work in the process of reconstruction. You should be no more overtaxed at this period than you were when an infant, or during childhood.

We do not grant this rest. We force the exhausted organization to work when it is unfit for work. We mistake our season for moulting, and consequent temporary weakness, for some form of disease. We then fix in our minds, through faith in evil, the idea of disease; so we construct a disease for ourselves. While Nature is trying to give us a new birth, rejuvenate us, and make us stronger, we defeat her purpose, and make ourselves weaker.

In the vast majority of cases, people cannot give themselves the rest Nature calls for. They must work on and on, from day to day, from year to year, to " make a living." That makes no difference as to the result. Nature's laws have no regard for man's systems. So fagged-out and ignorantly disobedient humanity fags on, and thousands " make a living," and toil and suffer and wear out, and die in misery on respectable beds of sickness.

In cases, habit is so strong that people cannot stop their work, or peculiar line of activity. They have no idea or capacity for resting spirit or body. They are miserable unless at work, and yet through growing weakness unhappy while at work,—like so many "house-wives," always complaining of being worked to death, yet unhappy if not at work.

Could these people once have mind and body brought into a condition approaching that of real rest, they would possibly be alarmed, and fear their powers were failing. They might for a time become sluggish, inert, and relatively inactive. That would be only because the strain being off mind and body, the spiritual power is using its force to recuperate and build anew. But you cannot work force in the outer, or physical, system, and the interior, or spiritual, system, at the same time. While one is at work, the other must stop.

Nature's great source of recuperation is rest. The land lying "fallow" gathers new force for growing grain. The mother whose mind and body are least taxed during gestation, gives birth to the healthiest child. The broken bone requires rest while being knit together.

By rest we mean rest of mind as well as body. Mental rest is as necessary as physical rest. Thousands of our race have no conception of mental rest, or a mind at ease. With them, worry, fret, uneasiness, and anxiety about something is a fixed habit. Rich or poor, it makes little difference. All this leads to exhaustion, decay, and disease. All this comes because men and women cannot as yet believe that they, as parts of God, or the Infinite Spirit, have spiritual power, which, if cultivated and trusted to, will supply all their needs, grant them perfect health, and give them delights they do not now dream of. Man is to see the day when he shall know that when he says, " I will do thus or so," and persist in that attitude of mind, that the thing he wills is being done,—that unseen forces are accomplishing the undertaking while his body sleeps, or, while awake, he is re-creating himself.

What we now call "death," is only the falling away from the spirit of the old body, before it has the power to put on the new one. Through ignorance and violation of spiritual law, our race has not yet given the spirit this opportunity. You cannot die. It is only your body that dies. You had a body in an existence previous to this. That died as others died before it. Your real life is the life of your mind, or spirit. You are not always to suffer the death of the body as in the past. A period is to come when your spirit will have so far matured its powers, that it can clothe itself gradually with a new physical body as the old wears away. Paul implied this possibility when he said, " The last great enemy which shall be destroyed is death."

When this law is known and followed, there will be results which would now be called miracles. Spirits (by which name we term all using, and in possession of, physical bodies) will have bodies for use on this stratum of life so long as they desire to use them; and such bodies being more perfect and symmetrical, will, as more perfect instruments, be better adapted to express such spirit's ever-grow-

ing powers. Your real self never loses any power.
It is only because of the giving out of the machine,
the body, that the spirit is unable to express that
power, even as the most skilful carpenter can do
little with a dull or broken saw.

MENTAL MEDICINE

THE first step toward both preventing and
curing any form of disease is to get out of
your mind the belief and error that your mental
force is growing less or can grow less. That is impossible. It may seem to grow less because of the
severity of your trials and afflictions. Bodies may
go to waste, but the unseen Force or mind using
those bodies never wastes or decreases. It may not
be able to act on the body. It may, through ignorance and lack of training in mental control, be
scattered as it is scattered in thousands of cases
where people's thoughts are drifting all about with
no power to fix those thoughts or that power on
any one thing for ten minutes. But the scatter-
brain's power or thought is all fastened to and
radiates from a centre. Only, he or she lacks power
to call it to that centre. The source of all strength
lies in the power of massing your thought or force
entirely on one thing.

The truth that you are a growing mind or Force
and MUST be an ever growing Force, and that this

Force can be self-applied to strengthen the body can never leave you. The presentation of this idea to you is for you a great spiritual power. It may at times be buried up and seemingly forgotten. You may at times waver and doubt and get discouraged Yet this truth will always come up again and assert itself, and reassert itself with greater and greater power, and finally proofs will come with such assertion and reassertion—proofs at first small but ever growing more convincing and ever increasing in number and importance—proofs as you find your maladies and weakness by degrees improving— proof as you find you do not take colds as readily as in years gone by.

The next step is to realize that the mind is the seat of all disease—that whatever thought is painful to the mind is a pain and cause of weakness to the body. If you are frightened your body feels the fright and is made weak. If you are angered your body shakes with that emotion. If you are in suspense or are hopeless or discouraged, the muscles do not feel or act as when you are bright or hopeful. Now you may for years have had fear or anger or suspense or discouragement acting on your body and it has weakened the body by degrees, and that weakness has affected some organ—eye, ear, stomach, lung, liver.

Resist IN MIND all that gives you pain or discomfort. Don't say in thought "It's too hot," or "It's too cold, I can't bear it." When you say that, in thought you surrender to the elements and their power over you and the pain they will bring your body is greater than ever.

Say in your silent thought "It is true my body

shrinks from this cold or this pain. But in my mind I will not shrink. I oppose the force that brings pain to my body. I defy it."

You are then ever building up a power to resist the effect of the elements on your body. Every moment you so in mind oppose heat or cold, or any pain or inconvenience whatsoever, is so much clear gain. Every thought you so put out is as real a resisting power as that which lies in the muscles of your arm to hold at bay a savage dog. Every such thought is an additional stone in the structure you are building up to protect yourself against evil.

Oppose then in thought the Devil in any form and he will flee from you. The Devil is in whatever tries to master you. If you do not so resist, he WILL temporarily MASTER you. You will never find a climate to suit you. It will always be too hot or too cold, or too something. You will find without such opposition the close, stuffy, overheated room still more uncomfortable. You will be borne down and overpowered by smells, by sights, by atmospheres.

It is by no means here implied that you must remain where surroundings or elements are unpleasant, any longer than is necessary. It is not implied that you should martyrize or torture yourself simply for the sake of enduring. It is not implied that you should FORCE on yourself what is unpleasant to mind or body. It is only implied that you should aim to master what is unpleasant, and so prevent its mastering you. There is no good gained by self-inflicted torture of any kind. That is often the mistake of the ascetic who deprives himself of all pleasures—of the hermit, who would make a merit of complete solitude—of the Hindoo, who gashes his flesh with knives or swings impaled on hooks. This is simply resistance carried too far. Because one can endure is no reason why he should endure, when endurance is no longer neces- sary. That is expending strength which might be used to far more profit in other directions. The ascetic in any form is as much enslaved to the idea of deeming pleasure a sin as the devotee of any single appetite is enslaved by that appetite. Self-conquest means simply self-control. It is right that the body as the instrument of the spirit should administer any form of pleasure which does not injure the spirit. It is not profitable that the body, as the instrument, should be able to ENFORCE any demand upon the spirit. The spirit is only safe when it can control and enforce its demands upon the body at any time, any place, and at any height of physical pleasure. The spirit is free ONLY when it can do this.

You may fear an event or an individual, and if you do not in mind resist that fear it will in some way wear on the body. You may in mind resist it for days and feel no change. Yet be sure that per- sistent attitude or attempt to bring courage kept up in your darkest, most depressing moments, when you seem to have no heart to meet anything, and it is hard to assert yourself even against the impertinence of a child—be sure that at last strength will come—a mood of mind will come in which you may see the thing you fear in a new light; you may see how needless was your fear, how much imagination magnified it, or you may see how puny are your opponents, and when in mind you feel above them, you are above them and must conquer them. You war in these states of timidity and depression far more with the unseen than the seen. You have working on your mind the Powers of Darkness, or, in other words, mischievous, annoying intelligences of the unseen side of life, who desire to defeat your purpose, who play upon some over-sensitive chord and so contrive to make a difficulty where none exists. Why are they allowed to do this? Because you must grow a force sufficient to overcome them. You cannot always be protected or you would have no force of your own. When through a prolonged struggle with some depressed or timid state of mind, force and strength at last comes to you, that force and strength is all your own. It can never leave you.

If your mind is in disorder, if you are thinking or trying to think of half-a-dozen things at once you want to do—if you don't know what to take hold of first and try to take hold of half-a-dozen things first, then your room will be in disorder, your desk and papers in disorder, and if this is a prevailing mood of mind your body will also suffer from some form of disorder, because the Force that does literally bind your body together is scattered. You are a bundle of sticks untied.

You can commence to tie them by setting in order a square inch or a square foot of your room or your desk—a corner of the room.

Don't try to do too much at once. Don't look at all there is to do. If you do it will give you that feeling of disgust for it all, weariness of it all, that is really a sickness of the mind and surely leads to sickness of body. If your eyes get a little weak don't run immediately for spectacles. Let the eyes rest a few months. No organ of the body is so strained as is the eye in the endeavour to read our fine print. The printer's limit for eye power is just as much as it can make out to see without spectacles. That is on the same basis as if you were given a load to carry which taxed the utmost power of your muscles to lift.

Make up your mind firmly that your eyesight must be as good as ever it was. In taking immediately to spectacles thousands unconsciously make up their minds that because the natural sight has failed, it has failed for the remainder of their lives. When you take to glasses you take to crutches for the eye. Then of course you use eye-crutches for the rest of your life. You do not reason or act in this way with a strained leg or foot. If you do seek the help of a crutch or a cane you are continually in mind wishing to do without that cane and trying from time to time to walk without crutch or cane.

The eye can be made weak by some weakness of the body and this weakness of the body was caused by some kind of trouble of the mind—either grief or worry or anxiety—about something, for all these states of mind exhaust the force of the body.

Rest enables an overtaxed stomach to recuperate itself. Rest enables an overtaxed muscle or limb to become as strong as ever. Why should not rest restore an overtaxed eye? It is the same unseen force that gives strength to all the body's organs. You do not rest the eye in wearing glasses. You do over-stimulate it through putting on an artificial lens for concentrating the light to make you see

1

which the natural lens has failed to do. It is an artificial stimulation for that organ as much as is the alcoholic artificial stimulation for the stomach to give it a temporary tone or get up an appetite, and you train your eye to lean and depend on the artificial stimulation. Of course, if you must read the fine print and in all shades of light, and your business compels you to, you must have the artificial aids, the glasses. But your necessities make no difference as to the result. A man can ruin his health as quickly in earning an honest support for his family as he can by imprudent exposure to damp air in highway robbery. The Law of Health is not even a respecter of motive and if you dash into a burning house to rescue a family, you may be as badly burned as the robber who dashes in with you for plunder.

If you have a slight deafness, keep your thought always against deafness. Can your mind, you ask, throw out an obstruction in the ear, an accumulation of the secretion peculiar to the ear? Your force or spirit throws off in time the outer covering or scab of a sore. It throws off continually the dead outer skin. When the mind can no longer use the body or the body as we say dies, there is no longer such casting off of dead matter from different portions and organs. Any sore that grows is because of lack of power or life in the body to bring to it life element or power. If you are educated to think a disease must increase, it will increase, because then your mind is working its force not to help its body but to encourage the idea that the body is falling to pieces. Your mind then feeds the disease.

More disease comes of lack of rest than any
other cause. Rest means rest for your mind as
well as body. Whatever rests the mind rests the
body. One means of rest comes of deep breathing
or taking long breaths with a second's interval between the inhaling and expelling of the breath.
The Cornish miner practises this when at each
blow with the sledge hammer, he makes the
ejaculation "Hah!" The sailor practises this when
hauling or hoisting, he utters a certain ejaculation
at the point where he has inflated his lungs to the
greatest possible extent, and then pauses a second
before expelling it with an exclamation. All who
work with him, time their lung exercise in accord
with the leader. The pause between the inhaling
and expelling the breath when you are doing no
physical work at all, rests the mind, because its
tendency is to bring your thoughts to a focus or
gather to one centre, and this, if only for a second,
when continued for a number of seconds, brings
your thoughts, your real self, more and more
together.

The other and material benefit of occasional
deep and measured or reposeful breathing is that
it brings more air into the lungs. Air is food as
well as grain. You increase the capacity of the
lungs to take in this food and you create a better
habit of breathing.

You are now suffering all manner of evil in unseen element, singly and alone. You are awakened
to the truth that the action or attitude or state of
your mind can benefit your health. But you can
receive great help from other minds acting co-
operatively and at the same time and in the same

place   If one mind can send in thought-element **a**
force to drive some form of disease from a person's
body, ten minds in unison can send a far greater
force. These ten minds in concentrated silent force
are as one mind or a unit, acting together on the
patient.

You benefit your friend very much when you
talk him over with another or others and wish him
well and keep his good qualities in the foreground
and his defects in the background. You then, out
of your minds, send him a current of element as
real as a current of electricity, which affects his body
beneficially and makes his brain the clearer to see
his own faults.

In the future and possibly the very near future,
when your friend is dangerously sick or afflicted
with some painful lingering malady, you will with
a few others, having sufficient Faith and apprehension of this Law, meet together in some quiet room
where the sun enters with the fresh force it sends
to this planet in the morning, and there clad in
your newest and freshest garments for an hour,
you will either send your best thought in silence to
that person, or if moved, speak of him, or if any
among you have the gift of song you may in that
way express sentiment and good-will for him, and
be sure you will come to know that in this way you
generate and send a power, a constructive power
and element to help that person. If practitioners
or people are immediately about them under whose
care and influence they are and whose methods
are different from yours, you will not in spoken or
unspoken thought antagonize them. You will send
only the thought and earnest desire that all having

nearest access to the patient may have their minds cleared as much as possible as to the right course to pursue, and you are in this peaceful co-operative attitude of mind sending the strongest of all the forces to the patient and those about him, for you have put yourself in the line of action with that High and Divine and powerful realm and current of thought and intelligence, which produce the most power.

It is to be known in the near Future by the wiser of the race that there is no gain in fighting for the Truth. Blows can in thought be sent in the air and they can do bodies harm. But when you have harmed a body by a blow, either of muscle or a blow from a silent antagonistic thought, what have you done to change the state of the person's mind whose body you may have destroyed? Nothing. If people's methods seem to you wrong and stupid, there is no gain but only harm in abusing the people or their methods. You bring on yourself in so doing the counter-current of hate and antagonism. Prove the wrong by showing a better way. If I have a better house than yours, I do not prevail on you to copy my house by abusing you for building such a house, or abusing your house. It is better to invite you to come into my house, look at it, and if you can see its superiority over your own, you may copy it, and if you can't see such superiority no further effort of mine can make you see until your eyes are wider opened.

Fatness comes through lack of Force to throw off an over secretion, on the same basis as there may not be enough Force to throw off the callous skin which Nature puts on to protect the foot from

the friction of a tight shoe. But the callous skin
may become as great a burthen or annoyance as an
excrescence, as the wearing leather it is meant to
protect against, and your spirit or force may not be
strong enough to throw it off. This causes the
corn which, as a remedy provided by Nature, becomes at last a source of more pain to the very
part it is intended to protect. A corn is a scab
which your spirit has not force enough to throw
off. If you cut this abnormal growth, you only
stimulate it to grow again, exactly as you stimulate the fruit tree to grow by trimming it of
superfluous branches. You concentrate on the
trimming process whether in the tree or the corn,
more of what force there is to renew branch or
corn.

●　　　●　　　●　　　●　　　●

During the youth of the body your spirit acts
with most force on that body. So wounds heal
quickly and all dead useless matter is more quickly
thrown off. The body like a vegetable has a growth
and life of its own, apart from your spirit or mind.
But it is a limited life—It has its growing, material
youth like a tree—its physical maturity or ripeness
like a tree, and then its decay like a tree, because
your spirit has not grown to sufficient power when
your body's maturity is reached, to call ever for
power to replenish that body with living unseen
element. You have not even known this was a
possibility. The proofs of this possibility are that
men of active fertile minds and strong wills do
unconsciously, in their desire and determination to
live as long as possible, call such power to themselves and such men do live longer than the average

lives. If they so live as long as they do, why should not human life be longer when this Law is recognized, and consciously and more intelligently exercised?

Magic implies results obtained without the use of physical agencies. Did we see more clearly we should find that all things done in the physical world are done through this power. Men and women having the stronger element of thought, move other men and women of lower and less powerful thought to their will. It is a power which no person can give or really teach another. It must be grown to by the individual even as in the physical world the infant grows to the strength of maturity. True, one person may as to this power, give another some suggestions and some little knowledge regarding its use. But if your knowledge in this respect is based and depends on what you may have received from others, then you have not struck the main source. That lies entirely in yourself. It needs but the persistent desire of two things.

First, to be in the path of exact Right and Justice to all, *including yourself.*

Second, to be able to believe in the Supreme Power as a reality from which you can by simple but imperative demand draw ever more and more of power (new ideas) to you and add it to you.

The sum and substance of all we have put out in these books is based on these two truths.

" Magic " is an intelligent use of the thought forces belonging to us and about us, exactly as the element of electricity not long since quite unknown is to-day utilized for many practical purposes.

This knowledge is open, not to all, but to those who can receive it. It is open to all who will not set their minds stubbornly against new ideas. Those who are so stubborn cannot be blamed. Their minds in their present condition cannot at once be changed to receive new ideas.

There can be no secrets to such as can receive. Nor can any secrets regarding this science be kept from such as are open to the truth. As you grow in spiritual knowledge new methods will be constantly opening to you to increase the power of your thought, to prevent its escape, to prevent adulteration and to use your power to the best advantage, first, for your own highest good, next, for that of others.

THE USE AND NECESSITY OF RECREATION

DIVIDE the word "recreation" in two parts, thus: re-creation and there is given it a clearer meaning. Recreation is a re-creative process for mind and body. In any healthy amusement we draw and build into ourselves a re-creative, recuperative, life-giving current of thought. Healthy amusement literally re-creates us. Life without amusement—life sad and serious, seldom, if ever, smiling—life plodding on in a monotonous rut and seeing and finding less and less to enjoy, is for the oody a de-creative and destructive process.

Re-creation not only throws off care, but adds to the capacity to resist care. Re-creation enables the mind to forget temporarily what is only an injury for it to remember. Re-creation adds new life to the body, because it brings new life to the mind, and life for the mind is life for the body. Re-creation gives strength to meet trial and difficulty. You do not so much want to be spared trial as you want that strength which shall cause you not to fear it. You do not want to run away from the person or the difficulty or the interview you dread as much as you want that state of mind when you meet that person, that difficulty, that terrible lion in your path, which shall not only rid you of all fear, but make the trial an entertainment for you.

Re-creation, and plenty of it, is one great source for getting this strength, for it is our so much dwelling on difficulties and the difficulty of getting our minds off our perplexities, caused in part through the great lack of colour or diversion in our lives, that add to those very troubles by making us weaker to resist them.

Were grown-up people able to play more in the spirit in which they played in their childhood, the more would they retain of the elasticity, litheness and vigour of childhood. Children in playing together do literally feed each other with a living element (the spirit of their play), and get from it a great stimulant and strength.

On the other hand, people drudging in companies and engaged in any effort in which they are not interested, feed each other with thought element, or spirit, heavy and sluggish in quality.

People so drudging, whose lives are monotonous, colourless and lacking in variety must become at last slow, heavy and sluggish in every movement of muscle, as well as mind.

Every effort we make and every kind of work we may have to do, be it digging in the garden or writing an essay, can be made a source of life-giving amusement or re-creation. No matter what you do it is the same force (*i.e.*, thought) which drives whatever part of the body you may use in the doing. If you dig, that force acts through the muscles used in digging. If you are an orator, the same force acts through your tongue to express the thoughts coming to you as you stand before your hearers. If a writer, the thought or force coming to you acts through arm and hand as put on paper.

Our so-called most trivial acts may be made sources of re-creation and pleasure. No act however small should be irksome. We have occasion a hundred times a day to do so-called little things wherein we are impatient in the doing. We snatch the coat from its hook. We reach for this or that article on our writing table, begrudging the time and effort it takes. In writing we shape our letters in a hurry and take no pleasure in giving them form or legibility. We are using our muscles constantly in some way which gives no pleasure. Every movement of muscle which gives no pleasure is a de-creative process. It adds its mite to the wearing out of the body. It begets the habit of impatience and unrest.

It is not work that kills people. It is the manner of doing it. Reposeful work is rest. But the science of repose reaches down to the crook of a finger, and a habit of order which will not neglect the proper place for a pin or a pen. Heaven is born out of the day of small things.

Perhaps you say, " If people should make phy sical effort in the slow, deliberate way you indicate, they would have very little done by the day's end."

To this we answer, that whatever is done in this mood would be well done and would not have to be done over again. But what is of far more importance in this reposeful, deliberate, and, it may be added, pleasure-giving way of performing physical acts, a great deal more at the same time would we be doing spiritually. The greatest results in life do not come of pushing material things about or using anything material. They will come to you, supposing you have a set purpose in view, in proportion as your thought or force works apart from your body on others favourable to that purpose. When you are in the current of hurried, fatiguing or irksome effort, that force works at great disadvantage. When you are in the current of reposeful, pleasure-giving effort, in every possible act your force works more and more on others night and day to your advantage. Results to you in material things will come quicker and quicker. New ideas will come faster.

Finally, you will gain ability to rest or gain strength in all effort, be it of any sort. You will as you call strength to you in any physical move ment reserve of it a little, instead of giving it all out in that effort. This is the secret of all physical effort when it is pleasant. It comes of mental or spiritual growth and not from any course of material training.

Especially the room sacred to ourselves should be the place above all for re-creative, reposeful, deliberate effort in the doing of all things. By such doing and in such calm frame of mind do we make a thought atmosphere in which our highest and best friends, unseen of the physical eye, can enter and mingle their thought with ours, so that our happiest moments will be realized there. And this realization of their presence and communion of mind will ever increase, when once we are in the re-creative mood of doing all things, so that finally all sense of loneliness shall depart. More, we can in such place and atmosphere receive the wisest suggestion and impression as to the course most proper to pursue in all our undertakings. You will then have fairly entered, when you can so enjoy what most people call "being alone," in that vast and unseen world of being, individuality and exist-ence, which lies closer to us than our doors. For it enters our doors. It is about us and all around us, and is surely to be reached and realized by some in our own time, as their minds so grow and refine as to be able to sense it, first faintly and feebly, but as time goes on its reality will be more and more apparent.

In ancient times there lived in oriental lands those of calm, contemplative and re-creative mood, who while acting little with the body accomplished great results through their spiritual power. A part of their secret lay in the cultivation of reposeful, re-creative effort in the doing of all things. The other part lay in their knowledge and trust in the

Supreme Power, and ever drawing more and more from that power.

In that world of to us unseen existence, many a poet, dramatist and writer has in mind entered and temporarily lived; as did Shakespeare. His creations to us are realities. Had they known better the laws of their being, could they have emerged from the domain of material thought and beliefs, they would at last have believed in their finer and spiritual senses, have more used and trusted them, and so going forward step by step, they would have shaken off the fetters of mortality, put on immortality and recognized what even they deemed fancies as truths. Their higher minds wrote down truths which their lower and material minds scorned, discredited and rejected afterward.

But the better period has dawned. Though its gray light as yet but tinges the sky, yet man does to-day stand in knowledge on the threshold of his more glorious and beautiful life. Let us not despise as trivial, the steps and methods by which only it can be realized; nothing is trivial.

Any effort ceases to be re-creative the moment it becomes wearisome. That is the time when our force or thought ceases to put new element into our mind or spiritual being.

If you come into the thought atmosphere of people who find pleasure in harmless recreation, you absorb of that atmosphere. It is life and life-giving element. It does good to mind and body. It builds up both and strengthens both.

When you re-create a mind, freshen it, get it for a time off a too much worn track of thought, physical effort or study, it is then cleared to receive new ideas. Inspiration does not come of memorizing or plodding or poring over books.

It comes of keeping the mind in a proper condition to receive newer thought than ever was printed in books, and newer device or invention than ever before was seen in the machine shop.

We are all of us dual. That is, we possess and use the mind of the body, and the other and higher mind which acts through the more powerful and far reaching spiritual senses.

The mind of the body, or that portion of our mind and force which acts directly on the body, often needs a certain limited, gentle and pleasing outlay of effort in the direction of seeing things of beauty or exercise of muscle, or hearing. Such outlay or exercise can keep it out of injurious currents of thought. For instance, many men get a certain rest in whittling. They can think more clearly while so engaged. In other words, the act of whittling concentrates their material mind on such exercise, while the other and higher mind and senses are liberated, and can go forth and act, and that certain repose a man feels while engaged in such act comes of the temporary liberation and exercise of his other and finer senses.

Thinking or getting new ideas does not come at all of trying to think. On the contrary, it comes of getting the mind in the most restful and contented mood. That is why some of my lady readers may get their best and most agreeable thoughts or mental moods while engaged without hurry, in their sewing or fancy work—or in any physical effort which you do not set out to do in just so many minutes, and care not whether it is finished this week or next. Work in this mood ceases to be work at all. It becomes play, and as we have said before, because it is worth twice saying, the gentle unstrained physical effort in getting the material mind on a certain track leaves the higher mind and senses more freedom to act in.

In time to come all the world's physical work will be done in this restful mood, and without hurry or straining to accomplish a certain amount in a certain time. Then all work will become as play. It will also be far better done. But far more results will come of such method of doing.

If you have any set purpose in view, and you have for the day done all physically you can to attain that purpose, stop further work. Rest, amuse yourself in some harmless way and re-create. You are then gathering force and putting it on that purpose. You are then sending force constantly to push your purpose forward.

But if you keep your mind ever on the rack and strain as regards that purpose—if you are making effort all the time with the body only because you think you must "be doing something," you are wasting force, driving the best results from you. Though you may gain small successes, they will not last and will be as nothing when compared with the greater and permanent result which comes of using and trusting your spiritual power.

Then if your material mind will set up a worry because things look dark or do not move fast enough, demand Faith of the Supreme Power.

The world's physical business, its building, its manufacturing is far too much hurried and strained. We act too much on the assumption that life is short, and so a great deal must be done in a short time. In a sense this is true. The very mental condition in which so many do business makes life short.

The race will realize in time to come that there is time enough to do all things reposefully and pleasantly, and that such mood of mind is one great factor in keeping the body strong and vigorous, and keeping that body far longer than its present average duration.

The young man who works all day at a trade is sometimes advised to go to the reading room, or a school of some sort in the evening, to "improve his mind." Does he "improve it," after having worked off so much force in the day time to work off more at night in the endeavour to fill himself with "facts," a part of which fifty years hence may have proved to be fiction?

There is re-creation in the study of any art when there is pleasure in such study. There is neither re-creation nor profit in the study of any art when we are tired or it becomes irksome. The moment you become tired is the moment to leave off. If you continue to paint or sew, or write your sermon, or if a lawyer, pore over your authorities, or as a mechanic continue your work when mind and body protest in some way against further effort, you have no longer fresh thought force or inspiration to put on such work. You have sundered your connection with such thought current. You have made con-nection with an inferior drudging, self-repeating current of thought. You are receiving of that thought element and putting it not only in your work but in your body. As a consequence you will leave off not only tired, but afterwards the very thought of your work will give you that peculiar mind sickness or disgust for it which always comes of over-strain and fatigue. So when next you take up such employment you may feel such disgust, for the reason that you re-absorb the tired thought you left in your work.

So when our business, our trade, our occupation, our art, be it what it may, ceases to re-create or give pleasure in the doing, or to be done with enthusiasm and zeal, it is not well done, and really does us and others more harm than good. It is the tired over-worked engineer whose exhausted faculties fail to recognize the danger signal and runs his train to destruction. It is the workman made careless through fatigue, who allows the flaw to go un-perceived in the shaft which breaks and possibly causes the steamer's wreck. It is the artist who paints mechanically, or the actor who acts me-chanically, with little or no love for his art or pleasure in its exercise, who never reaches the top rounds.

Up to a certain age, varying somewhat as to condition in life, the child is always learning some-thing new—some new game or sport. This is always giving it new life. If you bring up a child where it has no opportunity to learn new things, it will be a little old man or woman at ten or twelve years of age. When the boy or girl or young man or woman is put into the harness of conventional life, of the hard, serious, earnest work of life as we call it (which should not be hard, serious work at all were life what it should be and what it will be), when the boy has learned his one trade or pro

K

fession and settled down to that and that alone, and the girl has also settled down in life as wife and mother and house-carer, and that alone, then it is that they commence to become sad and serious, sober and careworn; and so life goes on till the end; and such minds exercised only in a rut, such spirit de-created through lack of re-creation, drop after middle age gradually into a corner, are pushed aside by the younger element, become of less and less use and importance in the social or business circle, until at last their worn-out bodies drop away from the spirit and are laid, as people say, "at rest," an assertion which may not be so readily believed as more is known of what life really means and what it involves.

Why is this? Because such minds are not re-created by the learning of some new thing—of some new source of re-creation—of some new source of rest whereby the thought or force is for a time diverted from some department of mind to another, some set of faculties to another, so that the lawyer in sailing his yacht shall be a rested and more powerful lawyer the next day—so that the matron in playing her part in the theatrical representation may return re-created and recuperated next morning to the government of that empire in embryo, her household—so that the preacher in his painting loses his preacher self in the paradise of form and colour, and returns to his pulpit with a fresh growth and shade of thought—grown in these periods of forgetfulness of preaching, and in this way should we all be makers of, and givers of new life to each other.

For when you amuse or interest me or compel

my attention or admiration by the display on your part of some great proficiency in music, in acting, in conversation, in skill and dexterity of muscle, you are proving and expressing some power and quality of God or the Infinite Spirit working through you, and in so centering my thought on one thing, you gather my scattered thought or spirit together, and in doing this you rest my spirit; and if you rest my spirit you rest my body with it; and if you rest my body you strengthen my body; and if you strengthen it you put in it the force or element to drive out disease.

When we cease to learn the new and take pleasure in such learning, the material part of us (the body) commences dying.

The ultimate of existence is a never ending course of learning and enjoying the new.

Paul says: " Rejoice evermore." It is the same as saying " play evermore." In other words, " Rejoice and receive pleasure in the never ending expressions of your spirit as they are one after another developed. Rejoice in your business, your trade, your profession. Rejoice in your walking, your driving, your eating, your painting, your music —in all you do."

But the physician might say here: "I take pleasure, to an extent, in the exercise of my profession. But sometimes it drives and wearies me. I am the slave of its demand, day and night. I am liable at any hour in the midst of my amusement, or rest, to be called to see a patient. How can I always rejoice? "

This question holds good with many professions.

Now, be your calling what it may, do you consider that you have full capacity and power for its exercise when you are tired, when vitality is at a low ebb, when your effort is strained, when you take little or no pleasure in its exercise? Are you then giving your best self, your best mind, your strongest power to your patient, your client, your patron in anything? Are you not, on the contrary, dealing out an inferior article?

"But I must go where my business or profession calls me," you answer, "whether I am physically or mentally fit to go or not. I cannot say to a midnight caller in case of sickness, 'I am unfit to give the patient the best of my skill now. He or she must wait till to-morrow.'"

Yes, you can when you trust more in that Supreme Power which stands by every soul in proportion to its trust in it. The greater success awaits those who trust it, and the greatest success means being master of your own time and independence to that extent that you can say "No" to any demand or tempting offer, when your highest conscience forbids its acceptance.

But all that interests and amuses our minds does not re-create.

That is an unhealthy and injurious taste which takes pleasure in spectacles of human suffering, be the suffering mental or physical. An audience which can look for hours on the spectacle of a human heart writhing in all the torments of jealousy or suspense or grief, is influenced by a grade of the same sentiment which once with pleasure saw the Christian captives suffering the same mental agony or fear as they were torn to pieces by wild beasts. Great talent is unquestionably shown in such representations, as great genius with the brush may expend itself in painting dead human flesh or in blood flowing freely from live human bodies from the axe of the executioner or the dagger of the assassin. That is amusement which does not re-create with healthy thought-element. It brings violence and fear and jealousy and all the lower order of thought more prominently to the minds of those who see it. It connects them with that domain or current of thought. It renders connection the more difficult with all that is quiet, beautiful, reposeful and constructive in nature. You absorb only elements of destruction and weakness after seeing a dramatic spectacle in which poison, the dagger, jealousy and revenge form the principal materials. You leave such a play worked up, exhausted, and the better fitted to connect yourself with what you call the Land of Dreams, with the same order of thought and action when your bodies are in the unconscious state we call sleep, and as a result you are the more apt to come back to and take up your physical instrument, your body, in the morning, unrefreshed, un-recreated, because during sleep your mind or spirit in its dual, and to your physical self, unconscious life, may have been sending to your body only the agitating violent destructive order of thought you saw last night at the tragedy.

     *   *   *   *   *

There is for all effort, whether as termed mental or physical, a higher and finer inspiration when the sexes mingle, as they should, in all games or diversions. Man is not improved, or so much benefited, or re-created when he goes by himself to his base-ball, his billiards, his bowling alley, his sailing, his driving. Left to himself in these amusements, and without the restraining, elevating and refining element of the other sex, he becomes the coarser. When man herds with man for long periods whether on ship-board, in armies or on frontier settlements, he becomes rough and coarse. When woman meets by herself, as she does in so many of our eastern towns and villages, where two-thirds of the men have "gone West," she becomes more narrow, gossipy, trivial, and is infected by that over prudishness, which seeing so much evil where evil is not, is the very essence of that evil which it most affects to fear.

Woman has as much nerve as man. She can be as cool in time of danger. Woman has quite as much vigour of muscle and endurance as man. The Sandwich Island women are rated as better swimmers than the men. Could a hod-carrier bound over the stage like a danseuse? In Vienna you may see a certain class of women carrying hods of brick and mortar up the long ladders like men. How many men would care to change places with a farmer's wife over her Monday's wash-tub, or with any one of the thousands of poor men's wives in this country, who are cooking, bed-making, house-sweeping, marketing, baby tending, with forty different things an hour for their minds? The more objects you have to expend thought or force upon in a given time—the quicker do you exhaust that force. Is woman really so much the weaker sex? Regard the girl acrobat on the trapeze, or the girl rider at the circus. Is she not as lithe and graceful on skates as the man? Regard the girl in her happier and "tomboy" days, when with the boy she has the glorious privilege of climbing trees, rolling down hay mows, roosting on barn ridge poles and sliding down cellar doors. Does she not enter into all these things with the same zest and enjoyment as the boy?

Does she not the more enjoy them when in company with the boy? Does she not as a rule cease to exercise what we will term the athletic side of her nature, when custom says she must cross over to her side of the house and act like a young lady and put on a dress which fetters her limbs? And what then? With less physical freedom, less of the natural and more of the artificial, less of open association, and, in so many cases, more of stolen interviews, are honesty and purity of mind increased? Are the evils, which society in so restricting the association of the sexes endeavours to prevent, really prevented?

Both men and women would be the stronger physically were all their re-creative effort in each other's company, for the reason that the elements flowing in thought from each to each give a certain strength and stimulation which is lacking when they are apart. In this restriction of the sexes which has crept upon us during the ages, and had its origin in the barbaric era when woman was held as a chattel, man has actually deprived himself of the only element which can refine him, and woman is likewise deprived of an unseen element which would strengthen her. It is this unnatural separation of the sexes which long custom has made an unconscious habit in so many phases of life, that begets the very evils it is intended to prevent.

THE ART OF FORGETTING

IN the chemistry of the future, thought will be recognized as substance as much as the acids, oxides, and all other chemicals of to-day.

There is no chasm betwixt what we call the material and spiritual. Both are of substance or element. They blend imperceptibly into each other. In reality the material is only a visible form of the finer elements we call spiritual.

Our unseen and unspoken thought is ever flowing from us, an element and force as real as the stream of water we can see, or the current of electricity we cannot see. It combines with the thought of others, and out of such combinations new qualities of thought are formed, as in the combination of chemicals new substances are formed.

If you send from you in thought the elements of worry, fret, hatred, or grief, you are putting in action forces injurious to your mind and body. The power to forget implies the power of driving away the unpleasant and hurtful thought or element, and to bring in its place the profitable element, to build up instead of tearing us down.

The character of thought we think or put out affects our business favourably or unfavourably. It influences others for or against us. It is an element felt pleasantly or unpleasantly by others, inspiring them with confidence or distrust.

The prevailing state of mind, or character of thought, shapes the body and features. It makes

us ugly or pleasing, attractive or repulsive to others.
Our thought shapes our gestures, our mannerism,
our walk. The least movement of muscle has a
mood of mind, a thought, behind it. A mind
always determined, has always a determined walk.
A mind always weak, shifting, vacillating, and uncertain, makes a shuffling, shambling, uncertain
gait. The spirit of determination braces every
muscle. It is the thought-element of determination
filling every muscle.

Look at the discontented, gloomy, melancholy,
and ill-tempered men or women, and you see in
their faces proofs of the action of this silent force
of their unpleasant thought, cutting, carving, and
shaping them to their present expression. Such
people are never in good health, for that force acts
on them as poison, and creates some form of
disease. A persistent thought of determination on
a purpose, especially if such purpose be of benefit
to others as well as to ourselves, will fill every nerve
with strength. It is a wise selfishness that works to
benefit others along with ourselves. Because in
spirit, and in actual element, we are all united. We
are forces which act and re-act on each other, for
good or ill, through what ignorantly we call "empty
space." There are unseen nerves extending from
man to man, from being to being. Every form of
life is in this sense connected together. We are all
"members of one body." An evil thought or act is
a pulsation of pain thrilling through myriads of
organizations. The kindly thought and act have for
pleasure the same effect. It is, then, a law of nature
and of science, that we cannot do a real good to
another without doing one also to ourselves.

To grieve at any loss, be it of friend or property, weakens mind and body. It is no help to the friend grieved for. It is rather an injury; for our sad thought must reach the person, even if passed to another condition of existence, and is a source of pain to that person.

An hour of grumbling, fret, or fear, whether spoken or silent, uses up so much element or force in making us less endurable to others, and perhaps making for us enemies. Directly or indirectly, it injures our business. Sour looks and words drive away good customers. Grumbling or hating is a use of actual element to belabour our minds. The force we may so expend could be used to our pleasure and profit, even as the force we might use with a club to beat our own body can be employed to give us comfort and recreation.

To be able, then, to throw off (or forget) a thought or force which is injuring us, is a most important means for gaining strength of body and clearness of mind. Strength of body and clearness of mind bring success in all undertakings.

It brings also strength of spirit; and the forces of our spirits act on others whose bodies are thousands of miles distant, for our advantage or disadvantage. Because there is a force belonging to all of us, separate and apart from that of the body. It is always in action, and acting on others. It *must* be in action at every moment, whether the body be asleep or awake. Ignorantly, unconsciously, and hence unwisely used, it plunges us into mires of misery and error. Intelligently and wisely used, it will bring us every conceivable good.

That force is our thought. Every thought of ours is of vital importance to health and real success. All so-called success, as the world terms it, is not real. A fortune gained at the cost of health is not a real success.

Every mind trains itself, generally unconsciously, to its peculiar character or quality of thought. Whatever that training is, it cannot be immediately changed. We may have trained our minds unconsciously to entertain evil or troubled thought. We may never have realized that brooding over disappointment, living in a grief, dreading a loss, fretting for fear this or that might not succeed as we wish, was building up a destructive force which has bled away our strength, created disease, unfitted us for business, and caused us loss of money and possibly loss of friends.

To learn to forget is as necessary and useful as to learn to remember. We think of many things every day which it would be more profitable not to think of at all. To be able to forget is to be able to drive away the unseen force (thought) which is injuring us, and change it for a force (or order of thought) to benefit us.

Demand imperiously and persistently any quality of character in which you may be lacking, and you attract increase of such quality. Demand more patience or decision or judgment or courage or hopefulness or exactness, and you will increase in such qualities. These qualities are real elements. They belong to the subtler, and as yet unrecognized, chemistry of nature.

The man discouraged, hopeless, and whining, has unconsciously demanded discouragement and hope-

lessness. So he gets it. This is his unconscious
mental training to evil. Mind is "magnetic," because it attracts to itself whatever thought it fixes
itself upon, or whatever it opens itself to. Allow
yourself to fear, and you will fear more and more.
Cease to resist the tendency to fear, make no effort
to forget fear, and you open the door, and invite
fear in; you then demand fear. Set your mind on
the thought of courage, see yourself in mind or
imagination as courageous, and you will become
more courageous. You demand courage.

There is no limit in unseen nature to the supply
of these spiritual qualities. In the words "Ask, and
ye shall receive," the Christ implied that any mind
could, through demanding, draw to itself all that
it needed of any quality. Demand wisely, and we
draw to us the best.

Every second of wise demand brings an increase
of power. Such increase is never lost to us. This
is an effort for lasting gain that we can use at any
time. What all of us want is more power to work
results, and build up our fortunes,—power to make
things about us more comfortable, to ourselves and
our friends. We cannot feed others if we have no
power to keep starvation from ourselves. Power to
do this is a different thing from the power to hold
in memory other people's opinions, or a collection
of so-called facts gathered from books, which time
often proves to be fiction. Every success in any
grade of life has been accomplished through spirit
ual power, through unseen force flowing from one
mind, and working on other minds far and near,
as truly as the force in your arm lifts a stone.

A man may be illiterate, yet send from his mind

a force affecting and influencing many others, far
and near, in a way to benefit his fortunes, while
the scholarly man drudges with his brain on a pit-
tance. The illiterate man's is the greater spiritual
power. Intellect is not a bag to hold facts. Intellect is power to work results. Writing books is but
a fragment of the work of intellect. The greatest
philosophers have planned first, and acted afterwards, as did Columbus, Napoleon, Fulton, Morse,
Edison, and others, who have moved the world,
besides telling the world how it should be moved.

Your plan, purpose, or design, whether relating
to a business or an invention, is a real construction
of unseen thought-element. Such thought-structure
is also a magnet. It commences to draw aiding
forces to it as soon as made. Persist in holding to
your plan or purpose, and these forces come nearer
and nearer, become stronger and stronger, and will
bring more and more favourable results.

Abandon your purpose, and you stop further
approach of these forces, and destroy also such
amount of unseen attracting power as you have
built up. Success in any business depends on the
application of this law. Persistent resolve on any
purpose is a real attractive force or element, drawing constantly more and more aids for carrying out
that resolve.

When your body is in the state called sleep,
these forces (your thoughts) are still active. They
are then working on other minds. If your last
thought before sleep is that of worry, or anxiety, or
hatred for any one, it will work for you only ill
results. If it is hopeful, cheerful, confident, and at
peace with all men, it is then the stronger force,

and will work for you good results. If the sun goes down on your wrath, your wrathful thought will act on others, while you sleep, and bring only injury in return.

Is it not a necessity, then, to cultivate the power of forgetting what we wish, so that our current of thought attracting ill, while our body rests, shall be changed to the thought-current attracting good?

To-day thousands on thousands never think of controlling the character of their thought. They allow their minds to drift. They never say of a thought that is troubling them, " I won't think of it." Unconsciously then they demand what works them ill, and their bodies are made sick by the kind of thought which they allow their minds to fasten on.

When you realize the injury done you through any kind of troubled thought, you will then commence to acquire the power of throwing off such thought. When in mind you commence to resist any kind of such injurious thought, you are constantly gaining more and more power for resistance. " Resist the devil," said the Christ, "and he will flee from you." There are no devils save the ill-used forces of the mind. But these are most powerful to afflict and torture us. An ugly or melancholy mood of mind is a devil. It can make us sick, lose us friends, and lose us money. Money means the enjoyment of necessities and comforts. Without these we cannot do or be our best. The sin involved in "love of money " is to love money better than the things needful which money can bring.

To bring to us the greatest success in any business, to make the greatest advance in any art, to

further any cause, it is absolutely necessary that at
certain intervals daily we forget all about that business, art, or cause. By so doing we rest our minds,
and gather fresh force for renewed effort.

To be ever revolving the same plan, study, or
speculation, or what we shall do or shall not do, is
to waste such force on a brain treadmill. We are
in thought saying to ourselves the same thing over
and over again. We are building of this actual,
unseen element, thought, the same cons'ructions
over and over again. One is a useless duplicate of
the other.

If we are always inclined to think or converse on
one particular subject, if we will never forget it, if
we will start it at all times and places, if we will
not in thought and speech fall into the prevailing
tone of the conversation about us, if we do not try
to get up an interest in what is being talked of by
others, if we determine only to converse on what
interests us, or not converse at all, we are in
danger of becoming " cranks," or " hobbyists," or
monomaniacs.

The "crank" draws his reputation on himself.
He is one who, having forced one idea and one
alone, on himself, has resolved, perhaps unconsciously, to force that idea on every one else. He
will not forget at periods his pet theory or purpose,
and adapt himself to the thought of others. For
this reason he loses the power to forget, to throw
from his mind the one absorbing thought. He
drifts more and more into that one idea. He sur-
rounds himself with its peculiar thought, atmosphere, or element, as real an element as any we
see or feel.

Others near him feel this one-ideaed thought, and feel it disagreeably; because the thought of one person is felt by others near him through a sense as yet unnamed. In the exercise of this sense lies the secret of your favourable or unfavourable "impressions" of people at first sight. You are in thought as it flows from you always, sending into the air an element which affects others for or against you, according to its quality, and the acuteness of their sense which feels thought. You are affected by the thought of others in the same way, be they far or near. Hence we are talking to others when our tongues are still. We are making ourselves hated or loved while we sit alone in the privacy of our chambers.

A crank often becomes a martyr, or thinks himself one. There is no absolute necessity for martyrdom in any cause, save the necessity of ignorance. There never was any absolute necessity, save for the same cause. Martyrdom always implies lack of judgment and tact in the presentation of any principle new to the world. Analyze martyrdom, and you will find in the martyr a determination to force on people some idea in an offensive and antagonistic form. People of great ability, though dwelling in one idea, have at last been captured by it. The antagonism they drew from others, they drew because they held it first in their own mind. "I come not with peace," said the Christ, " but a sword." The time has now come in the world's history for the sword to be sheathed. Many good people unconsciously use swords in advising what they deem better things. There is the sword (in thought) of the scolding reformer, the sword of dislike for others because they won't heed what you say, and the sword of prejudice because others won't adopt your peculiar habits. Every discordant thought against others is a sword, and calls out from others a sword in return. The thought you put out, you receive back of the same kind. The coming empire of peace is to be built up by reconciling differences, making of enemies friends, telling people of the good that is in them rather than the bad, discouraging gossip and evil speaking by the introduction of subjects more pleasant and profitable, and proving through one's life that there are laws, not generally recognized, which will give health, happiness, and fortune, without injustice or injury to others. Its advocate will meet the sick with the smile of true friendship, and the most diseased people are always the greatest sinners. The most repulsive man or woman, the creature full of deceit, treachery, and venom, needs your pity and help the most, for that man or woman, through generating evil thought, is generating pain and disease for himself or herself.

You find yourself thinking of a person unpleasantly from whom you have received a slight or insult, an injury or injustice. Such thought remains with you hour after hour, perhaps day after day. You become at last tired of it, yet cannot throw it off. It annoys, worries, frets, sickens you. You cannot prevent yourself from going round and round on this same tiresome, troublesome track of thought. It wears on your spirit; and whatever wears on the spirit, wears on the body.

This is because you have drawn on yourself the other person's opposing and hostile thought. He is

L

thinking of you as you are of him. He is sending you a wave of hostile thought. You are both giving and receiving blows of unseen elements. You may keep up this silent war of unseen force for weeks, and if so, both are injured. This contest of opposing wills and forces is going on all about us. The air is full of it.

To strive, then, to forget enemies, or to throw out to them only friendly thought, is as much an act of self-protection as it is to put up your hands to ward off a physical blow. The persistent thought of friendliness turns aside thought of ill-will, and renders it harmless. The injunction of Christ to do good to your enemies is founded on a natural law. It is saying that the thought or element of good-will carries the greater power, and will always turn aside and prevent injury from the thought of ill-will.

Demand forgetfulness when you can only think of a person or of any thing with the pain that comes of grief, anger, or for any cause. Demand is a state of mind which sets in motion forces to bring you the result desired. Demand is the scientific basis of prayer. Do not supplicate. Demand persistently your share of force out of the elements about you, by which you can rule your mind to any desired mood.

There are no limits to the strength to be gained through the cultivation of our thought-power. It can keep from us all pain arising from grief, from loss of fortune, loss of friends, and disagreeable situations in life. Such power is the very element or attitude of mind most favourable to the gain of fortune and friends. The stronger mind throws off the burdensome, wearying, fretting thought, forgets it, and interests itself in something else. The weaker mind dwells in the fretting, worrying thought, and is enslaved by it. When you fear a misfortune (which may never happen), your body becomes weak; your energy is paralyzed. But you can, through constantly demanding it, dig out of yourself a power which can throw off any fear or troublesome state of mind. Such power is the high road to success. Demand it, and it will increase more and more, until at last you will know no fear. A fearless man or woman can accomplish wonders.

That no individual may have gained such amount of this power, is no proof that it cannot be gained. Newer and more wonderful things are ever happening in the world. Thirty years ago, and he who should assert that a human voice could be heard between New York and Philadelphia would have been called a lunatic. To-day, the wonder of the telephone is an every-day affair. The powers still unrecognized of our thought will make the telephone a tame affair. Men and women, through cultivation and use of this power, are to do wonders which fiction has not or dares not put before the world.

CULTIVATE REPOSE

REPOSE is a quality. It may be cultivated and gradually attained by allowing the mind to dwell upon it. Fix the word in your brain. Paste

It up there figuratively. Paste it somewhere about you literally. You want the thought in your mind. You want to plant it there so that it may grow. It will then take root and grow. As it grows, you will, despite ten thousand failures, find yourself on the gain. You will correct yourself many, many times in hasty doings, but each correction will bring you though ever so little, nearer the mark. If you are annoyed at your failures, so much the better. That shows you know your defect.

It is a training also where the school is ever by you. It can be practised as soon as you rise in the morning, in the putting on of your apparel, in your walk, in your eating, in your opening and shutting of doors. No act is beneath it. No act is above it. Each act so done lays up for you its little quota of capital—until at last the habit becomes " second nature," and the forced schooling merges into an involuntary one.

There is a law which causes the sound sleep of childhood. There is another law, governing the unsound sleep often common to middle age, if not sooner. A law governs everything. A law governs the decay of a building; the decay of a body; the decay of a tree as well as the healthy growth of a tree.

We do not at night lay our real selves down to rest. We lay down only the body, the instrument we use in the material domain of expression to be recuperated. If the spirit gains renewed force while away from the body, as it should, it will return with such force to act on the body in the morning, if we realized the highest condition of sleep.

There are two kinds of sleep. There is a sound healthy sleep, which strengthens and refreshes the body, and an unsound, feverish, restless sleep whereby the body awakes with very little strength. When you are awake, your spirit or thought is acting on the body or using it. If it so acted all the time, it would soon wear out the body as sleeplessness does wear it. When you sleep, your spirit or thought still acts, thinks, works, but apart from the body. It can so act in a healthy or unhealthy realm of mind. If in a healthy realm of mind, it will send the body healthy element in thought to repair or recuperate it. If it goes to an unhealthy realm, it will send the body only unhealthy element. Whether it goes to a healthy or unhealthy territory of spirit depends entirely on your condition of mind before retiring. If the "sun goes down on your wrath " or irritability or hatred of others, your mind during the night will send your body still the unhealthy elements of wrath, hatred or irritability. Or if your spirit is discouraged, despondent and hopeless, it will send to the body the same order of element.

You are working or making effort whenever you think. You do not want to do work of any kind when you go to bed. In some cases when we lie down, the mind becomes more active than ever and fills immediately with plans and schemes or anxieties or worryings. That tires the body and causes restlessness and tossing and wakefulness for hours. The mind is then more active, because it is momentarily diverted from any bodily effort.

You will make up your mind to dismiss all thought whatever on retiring, and think only of repose. Keep the word "repose" in your mind on going to bed. The word brings the idea of rest. This will gradually change the attitude or direction of your thought, and connect you with the element of rest and repose. You may not be successful at first in bringing immediate sleep. You may have this mental habit of brain working for years to conquer. You will by degrees change your mind to the reposeful condition as you persevere. It may require months before you see any change for the better. But when once you have conquered wakefulness, you will never have your work to do over again. You cannot at once change any mental habit, the growth possibly of years all at once, any more than you can at once change a habit of body, a mannerism or peculiar gesture, or a peculiar walk, or a peculiar manner of speech.

If your mind is from any cause very much disturbed during the day, it sends to the unconscious body or unconscious physical existence the same disturbing thought element at night. What mood your mind is most in during your waking hours that mood is your mind in when the body sleeps. The mind never sleeps, any more than electricity sleeps; any more than the element which the sun sends us (the cause of light and heat after reaching this planet) sleeps. The child is a spirit coming into this physical life again with a new body. The memory of all its troubles in its previous existence is fortunately blotted out. It is well in this our incomplete state and with so little power to rule our minds and turn them from the unpleasant, that we do not know what we may have suffered in a past existence. If we did, we might begin at the age of

two years with the troubles we had at three-score
and ten of the last life.

Up to a certain age the child has a perfect trust
in its parents to supply it with food, clothing and
shelter. When it is obliged to provide for itself the
trouble begins—the trouble and work it carries
when grown up, to bed with it. Then it trusts
hardly anything. That may be the cause of all
our trouble, wakefulness included.

It means really little or nothing to say "Trust in
God," and little wonder, for it is said so much by
people who do not trust in God, but in their own
relatively weak physical efforts—or in the weak or
imperfect reason that is based entirely on physical
surroundings.

When the Christ showed the little trusting, undisturbed child to the probably worrying, fretting
and possibly sleepless, Elders of Judea and said
" Unless you become in mind as free from care as
this child and learn to trust for all you want to an
Infinite All-Pervading Force or Father, you cannot
enter the Kingdom of Heaven " (which is an entirely
mental kingdom), he meant that the human thought
when fixed persistently on a thing or purpose sets
in motion the unseen force to accomplish that purpose, and that this is the Infinite Force or God
working through us.

He meant that if you have an earnest desire to
do anything which will with yourself, benefit others,
or to be anything in the domain of Art—whether
orator, actor, writer, painter, inventor—one of the
world's movers in some way—that earnest, persistent desire is the great unseen Force, evolving
out of yourself as a part of God or the Infinite

Power which rules all things—to push you on to success, and the more you trust to this desire, and after making all reasonable plan and effort toward material support, you leave off worrying and fretting as to that material support, the stronger is the Force for accomplishment that is acting for you.

He meant when he said, " Come unto me all ye that are heavy laden and I will give you rest," come to me as one representative of this great and Incomprehensible Law of Nature. He would say if here to-day, as illustrative of this Law: I have in mind a certain thing to do. I trust to that strong desire to do it. I ask or pray for wisdom to direct my doing. I use my body in the doing as my spirit leads or impels me, and if I cannot see the way clear, still I trust to the desire or power of the Infinite, a part of which I am, knowing that the Force I have set in motion is working for me night and day. So when I lie down to sleep I do so with as perfect a trust and faith that this Force will some where and in some place have put me further ahead toward my accomplishment by to-morrow, as this child has that its parents will provide for it to-morrow, and in such trust and faith the spirit leaves the body and goes to some realm where there is even greater trust and faith and knowledge and proof and apprehension of the Laws, and sends from that realm by the thought link connecting it with the sleeping body more and more in thought element of trust and faith, and power, and rest.

When we gain this trust and faith, as we can and shall, through more and more proofs of the reality of the power on which it will be based, we have gained the most important factor for sleep, and healthy sleep. And the incessant desire or aspiration to have such trust will bring it.

The element the Sun sends us is the force giving life to all forms of what we call organized matter on our planet. Acting on the life of the seed in the earth it brings it that renewal of Force, which starts it into renewed life.

Our bodies have the most Force in the morning, because then the tide of the Sun's Force is coming toward us. Our spirits absorb that Force, and the strength so given to the spirit is communicated to the body. In the afternoon and evening that portion of the Earth on which we live is turned away from the Sun Force. It no longer meets and affects us as in the morning. For this reason there is less strength and vigour of mind and body in the latter part of the day. For this reason is the tendency in most birds and beasts to rest their bodies at night. Night is the time for repose of the body, because of the absence of that element sent from the Sun, which is the great stimulator to life of all things on this planet.

We are most in the line of Natural Law when we do the work requiring most exertion in the morning. We have then the most benefit of the Force coming to the Earth. In the evening it is better to let the mind dwell on light and harmless recreation, to reverie if so we are inclined, to easy effort which does not tax the faculties to the utmost. And in such a state of mind we are more easily enabling it to cease acting on the body when we retire.

People do work in various ways in the evening and accomplish a great deal. But they pay a heavy price at last. They so fix their thought on one business or one line of effort that they cannot get their thought out of that groove. Their minds run in the same rut be the body asleep or awake. You rest most in turning thought from one line of effort to another. Carrying any business or study in the mind all the time, day and night, morning and evening, does not really advance that business as much as forgetting it at intervals and letting the mind rest, as you allow your muscles to rest after any physical exertion. Mind allowed to rest gains new ideas and new Force to carry out ideas. A new idea is worth waiting for. But if now, as is so often the case, business and work are carried into the latter part of the day as well as far into the night, the mind, even when the body is laid down to rest, cannot readily, if at all, detach itself from that train of thought, and even when it does and the body's physical senses become unconscious, the other, the finer or spiritual senses, are working still on the same line of action. We gain thereby little or nothing. We send back to the body only old worn out second-hand ideas, which is second-hand life. We take up the body again in the morning for use, with only the same old set of thoughts, views, plans, and worries we had yesterday, because when the body became unconscious our spirits went into the same thought element, a realm whither we directed them when the weary eyes closed.

What is the remedy? More recreation. More variety of occupation. More variety of colour in our lives. More selves in our one self. To attain the highest and happiest life we need to have two and possibly three, if not four lives in one—to be merchant in the morning and artist or yachtsman or something else in the afternoon, and in the second life forget for the time all about the first, and in such forgetfulness rest the first life or set of faculties, recuperate them, refresh them, and go back to business, or art or science, or any occupation next day with more force, plan, idea, thought to put in it, as do many of our most successful men of business, who leave their offices at an early hour of the afternoon and may be seen driving on the Boulevard or otherwise recreating themselves.

If you sleep with another person whose mind is more disturbed than yours, who is worried, fretted, despondent, or irritable, your thought being more or less set on that person, so your spirit will be attracted or drawn at night to that person's lower province of mind. You are then dragged down on the lower level of that person's night life. Your spirit does not then absorb such healthful element as it would did you sleep alone. It sends then to your body the other person's more disturbed thought element. Your spirit also returns to its body in the morning adulterated more or less with the element it has absorbed of that other person's thought, and has far less power to act on its body.

The harm that comes to the young person sleeping with an old one is when the older person's mind is letting go of life, taking less and less interest in things about it, erroneously deeming it too old to learn, believing that because the body is wearing out all life is worn out. What life the younger person gains through going to a fresher domain of thought is to an extent absorbed by the older, who thus unconsciously appropriates the younger one's stimulation.

Bear in mind that our real youth is not dependent on the age of the body—that youth implies never-ceasing vigour and activity of mind and more and more interest and effort in human affairs, more and more aspiration, and it is among the certain possibilities of the life coming to this planet that this state of mind once fixed on, will constantly re-invigorate, re-cuperate and re-juvenate the body.

The body has a certain life of its own separate from the spirit, whose instrument it is. Like a plant, it has its youth, maturity and decay. Its physical life in its earlier existence is an aid to the life and vigour of your spirit. That youthful physical life is an aid to your spirit, as any material remedy may bring a certain force to aid the spirit to throw off disease or weakness. But the body's aid in this respect only lasts for a certain time if not renewed by the power of mind or spirit, and if there is no knowledge of such power to renew, the body as a material construction like any other material construction, must fall to pieces.

There is a great deal of unconscious belief in untruths. You will find from time to time that you have during all of this physical life believed implicitly in some falsehood. You have never questioned its truth, never thought of questioning it. You may be surprised at the number of errors so credited by you as they continue to crop up.

Your unconscious, unquestioning belief made these untruths as regards their effect on your life all the stronger. If you live firmly believing in an

error, that error will bring a blight of some kind
into your life. It is this firmly held belief in untruths that causes every kind of sickness and
trouble for our race. "The truth," says the Bible,
"shall make you free,"—free from all pain and
trouble.

As soon as we commence to question any of
these long held untruths, their reign is over. Disturbance commences. That is because it is being
kicked out of your mind.

You may when a child have been taught to believe in a Bug-a-boo of some kind. You may have
feared in consequence to go alone in the dark.
You believed it for a time implicitly. Then with
years, you doubted, and you ceased finally to believe
it in the form it was first presented to you.

When you believed firmly in the Bug-a-boo, the
thought of it when alone in the dark caused you
unpleasant physical sensations. Your flesh "crept"
or your hair rose on end, or you became weak and
trembling. That is, you were made in a way, sick,
by the thought of a thing which had no existence.

If some thoughtless person had simulated to
you in the dark the Bug-a-boo or ghost, your body
might have been still more strongly affected. The
physical disturbance would have been greater. You
might have been "scared to death" or scared into
loss of reason, as children have been in similar
circumstances. That is, you might have lost your
body or your reason, through the idea of a thing
which had no real existence.

The Bug-a-boos held firmly in belief by grown
up persons, act on the body in a precisely similar
manner. Misconception as regards an effort of the

spirit to regenerate the body makes of that effort a Bug-a-boo, which finally works on the mind to destroy the body.

The spirit demands rest of the body. It wants all its force used in building it anew. It makes such demand of the stirring man of business, who has been actively engaged for years. The demand may come in the form of sluggishness or inactivity of some sort.

As the regenerating process goes on we shall become in our habits and modes of living more natural. In all natural things in the animal and vegetable, undisturbed and uncultivated by man, do we find the most perfect expression of the infinite mind, although these are not perfected expressions. Nothing in the universe is perfected or finished. Everything is growing ever to increased perfection. And this growth must be as the Infinite Mind wills, and not as man wills. Wherever man tampers with the natural he makes imperfection and deformity.

Taking the wild and tamed bird, we see the difference between the artificial and unnatural, and the natural and healthy life. The wild bird is as God made it. As man meddles with it, he deprives the bird in time of strength, agility, beauty, and a great deal of intelligence.

Intelligence, instinct and spirituality mean the same. They imply a knowledge coming not from books but from the Infinite Mind. This knowledge in greater or less degree, is in all forms of matter. It is in the mineral, the plant, the worm, the animal to man. It is not in all men alike. It is in no man to-day as it will be in the man of the future. It will be given to the man of the future so that he will be an immortal. That man will realize a happiness and peace of mind so vainly sought for to-day, so seldom found. He will realize a happiness undreamt of to-day.

He will realize this increasing happiness, because of seeing clearly that there is an exhaustless force, mind and wisdom moving in everything, himself included, and that all he has to do to attain lasting and ever increasing happiness is to commit himself to this power for good, trust to it, and be carried from one condition of pleasure to another.

Have all our inventions and advance in civilization made the race any happier or healthier? Is not the struggle for existence about as hard as it was one hundred or one thousand years ago? Are not disease and suffering still rampant? Are not loss, bereavement and disappointment met on every side? How many can say, " My life is free from care, or anxiety, or jealousy, or discontent. My life is a dream of content and bliss. My life from the sun's rising until its setting is a series of pleasant moments. And more, I know that my days of pleasure will not only continue, but that my quiet internal content will ever increase. I have no anxiety for the morrow, for I have proven this great power. It has made my past days pleasant, and I am equally certain it will my future?"

Trusting, then, to this power, and being carried by it, man, becoming more than mortal, will have no occasion to sow or reap, or invent machinery—any more than does the wild bird, unhampered by such incumbrances. His spiritual growth will give him powers which shall do away with these present necessities.

In this regenerating process our spirit or higher self will demand of the body more sleep. It will demand that the night be devoted wholly to sleep.

Because when daylight prevails that is the time best adapted for physical expression. The material world is then most moved by the material force coming from the sun.

When that force is withdrawn and darkness prevails another power prevails. That is a spiritual power which can feed the material when the material activities are quiet.

When you retire at night with a desire to be free from the mood of anger or anxiety, and with a silent demand of the Supreme Power that you shall be led into the way of the highest wisdom and happiness, you are in the way of having that quality of sleep which shall most benefit you.

Healthy repose at night will give healthy repose by day. Repose is the mental condition most needed by our race. Repose is not sluggishness, inertia or laziness. Repose gives pleasure in the doing of all things. Repose brings more strength in the doing of all things. Repose casts out exhaustion. Repose makes all work agreeable. Repose frees all labour from irksomeness. Repose means the steady nerve and hand, whether that of the draughtsman, the marksman, or the rigger working from the dizzy height of the ship's mast.

Repose does all things with an elaborate and loving care.

Repose will ultimately make you lose all sense of time. It is that weariness born of exhaustior which makes men and women sometimes say: "What shall we do to kill time? How tedious are the hours!"

Repose is a healthy, quieting stimulus ever flowing from the spirit near the Supreme Mind to the body. It gives permanently that mental rest which men seek and get from alcohol and opiates. But the pleasure derived from those agencies is transient, often spasmodic, and liable to that reaction which carries down to gloom as high as it has lifted to bliss. Repose keeps you on a serene level of happiness, and as you continue to invoke the Supreme Mind, carries you gradually to a condition still higher and happier, and so ever on and on.

Repose makes you company for yourself, welcome always to yourself, agreeable always to yourself. When that is your prevailing mood, you are always agreeable to others as are they to you. You cease then to be dependent on others for company. But in so ceasing you draw the best from others, give them of your best, and therefore never lack for company.

Repose brings plan and idea for enduring success and force to accomplish it. Success means far more than mere money getting. The success of to-day often brings wealth and fame without happiness. Is that a success when a man can call an empire his own, and his body, the only instrument by which he holds it, has not ten years life in it?

I do not assert here that merely retiring early would prove a panacea for all the ills of the race. Nor that turning night into day is the cause of all the ills of the race.

M

But I do assert that an unhealthy spiritual condition tends to turn night into day, and that as the spirit becomes more healthy and natural, it will prompt us to sleep, while Nature, drawing the veil of darkness over the material world, signals thereby to the material world the time to cease from material activity.

Repose opens more and more the spiritual faculties, the finer perceptive powers, the faculty of seeing beauty and use in the many neglected things about us.

LOVE THYSELF

CHRIST'S precept says: " Love thy neighbour as thyself." Some people incline to forget the last two words " as thyself," and infer that we should love others even better than ourselves. So far has this idea been carried that it has led in cases to entire sacrifice and neglect of self so that good may be done to others.

There is a justifiable and righteous love for self.

There can be no true spiritual growth without this higher love for self. Spiritual growth implies the cultivation and increase of every power and talent. It means the making of the symmetrically developed man and woman. Spiritual growth fostered by unceasing Demand of the Supreme Power will bring power to keep the body in perfect health to escape pain and disease—and will eventually carry man above the present limited conditions of mortality.

The higher love of self benefits others as well as ourselves.

When we love a person, we send that person our quality of thought. If it is the aspiring order of thought it is for that person a literal element and agency of life and health, in proportion to his or her capacity for absorbing and assimilating it. If we think meanly of ourselves—if we are beggarly in spirit—and are content to live on the bounty of others, if we care little for our personal appearance—if we are willing to get money by questionable means—if we believe there is no Supreme and overruling Power, governing our lives by an exact law, that everything is left to chance, and that life is only a scramble for existence, we send in thought such beliefs to that person, and if our love is accepted it is only a means to drag down instead of a power to elevate.

How can we send the highest love to another if we do not have it for ourselves? If we are careless and unappreciative of the body's great use to us— if we never give it a thought of admiration or gratitude for the many functions it performs for us—if we regard it with the same indifference that we may have for the post to which we hitch a horse, we shall send that same quality of sentiment and thought to the person we think most of, and the tendency of such thought on them will be to generate a similar disregard for themselves.

Either they will do this, or seeking light of the Infinite, they will find themselves obliged in self-protection to refuse the love we send them, because of its coarser and grosser quality.

This is sometimes the error of mothers, who say: "I don't care for myself so that my son or daughter's welfare is assured. I give and devote my whole life to them."

This means, "I am content to grow old and unattractive. I am content to slave and drudge so that my children may receive a good education and shine in society. I am an old and decaying weather-beaten hulk and can't hold together much longer, and the best use I can make of myself is to serve as a sort of foot-bridge for them in the shape of nurse, grandmother, and overseer of the nursery and kitchen, while they are playing their parts in society."

The daughter receives this thought with the mother's inferior self-neglecting love. She absorbs it and assimilates it. It becomes part of her being. She lives it, acts it out, and thirty years afterwards is saying and doing the same and laying herself upon the shelf with the rest of the cracked teapots for her daughter's sake.

Ancestral traits of character as bequeathed and transmitted from parent to child are the thoughts of the parent absorbed by the child.

When in thought, desire and aspiration we make the most of what the Infinite has given us (inclusive of these wonderful bodies), we shall have continual increase, and such increase will overflow of its own accord and benefit others.

The highest love for self means justice to self. If we are unjust to ourselves we shall be unavoidably unjust to those to whom we are of the greatest value. A general who should deprive himself of necessary food and give all his bread and meat to a hungry soldier, might in so doing weaken his body, and with his body weaken his mental faculties, lessen his capacity for command, thereby increasing the chances for the destruction of his entire army.

What is most necessary to know and what the Infinite will show us as we demand, is the value we are to others. In proportion to our power for increasing human happiness, and in proportion as we recognize that power, will the needful agencies come to us for making our material condition more comfortable.

No man or woman can do the best work for themselves or others, who lives in a hovel, dresses meanly, and starves the spirit by depriving it of the gratification of its finer tastes. They will always carry the atmosphere and influence of the hovel with them, and that is brutalizing and degrading. If the Infinite worked on such a basis would the Heavens show the splendour of the Suns? Would the fields reflect that glory in the myriad hues of leaf and flower, in plumage of bird and hue of rainbow?

What in many cases prevents the exercise of this higher love and justice to self is the thought, " What will others say, and how will others judge me if I give myself what I owe to myself?" That is, you must not ride in your carriage until every needy relative has a carriage also. The general must not nourish his body properly because the hungry soldier might say that he was rioting in excess. When we appeal to the Supreme and our life

Is governed by a principle, we are not governed either by fear of public opinion or love of other's approbation, and we may be sure that the Supreme will sustain us. If in any way we try to live to suit others we never shall suit them, and the more we try, the more unreasonable and exacting do they become. The government of your life is a matter which lies entirely between God and yourself, and when your life is swayed and influenced from any other source you are on the wrong path.

Very few people really love themselves. Very few really love their own bodies with the higher love. That higher love puts ever-increasing life in the body and ever-increasing capacity to enjoy life.

Some place all their love on the apparel they put on their bodies; some on the food they put in their bodies; some on the use or pleasure they can get from their bodies.

That is not real love for self which gluts and gourmandizes with food or which keeps the body continually under the influence of stimulants. It is not a real love for self which indulges to excess in any pleasure to be obtained from the body. The man who racks and strains his body and mind in the headlong pursuit of pleasure or business, loves that business or art unwisely. He has no regard for the instrument (the body) on which he is dependent for the materialization of his ideas. This is like the mechanic who should allow a costly tool by which he is enabled to do rare and elaborate work, to rust or be otherwise injured through neglect.

That is not the highest love for self which puts on its best and cleanest apparel when it goes out to visit or promenade and wears ragged or soiled clothes indoors. That is love of the opinion or approbation of others. Such a person only dresses physically. There is a spiritual dressing of the body when the mind in which apparel is put on is felt by others. Whoever has it in any degree will evidence it in a certain style of carrying their clothes which no tailor can give.

The miser does not love himself. He loves money better than self. To live with a half-starved body, to deny self every luxury, to get along with the poorest and cheapest things, to deprive self of amusement and recreation in order to lay up money, is surely no love for the whole self. The miser's love is all in his money bags, and his body soon shows how little love is put in it.

Love is an element as literal as air or water. It has many grades of quality with different people. Like gold, it may be mixed with grosser element. The highest and purest love comes to him or her who is most in communion and oneness with the Infinite Mind and ever demanding of the Infinite Mind for more and more of its wisdom. The regard and thought of such a person is of great value to any one on whom it is directed. And that person will of that wisdom be wisely economical of his sympathy for others, and put a great deal of this higher love into himself in order to make the most of himself.

Some people infer from their religious teachings that the body and its functions are inherently vile, and depraved; that it is a clog and an incumbrance to any higher and more divine life; that it is corruptible "food for worms," destined to return to dust and moulder in the earth. It has been held that the body should be mortified, that the flesh should be crucified and starved and subjected to rigorous penance and pains for its evil tendencies. Even youth with its freshness, beauty, vigour and vivacity has been held as almost a sin, or as a condition especially prone to sin.

When a person in any way mortifies and crucifies the body either by starving it or dressing meanly, or living in bare and gloomy surroundings, he generates and literally puts in the body the thought of hatred for itself. Hatred of others or of self is a slow thought-poison. A hated body can never be symmetrical or healthy. The body is not to be refined and purged of the lower and animal tendencies by being made responsible and continually blamed for these sins—by being counted as a clod and an incumbrance, which it is fortunate at last to shake off. Religion, so called, has in the past made a scapegoat of the body, accused it of every sin, and in so doing and thinking filled it with sin. As one result of this the professors of such religion have suffered pain and sickness. Their bodies have decayed, and death has often been preceded by long and painful illness.

"By their fruits ye shall know them." The fruits of such a faith and condition of mind prove error in it.

There is a mind of the body—a carnal or material mind—a mind belonging to the instrument used by the spirit. It is a mind or thought lower or cruder than that of the spirit.

But this mind of the body need not, as has been held, be ever at war with the higher mind of the spirit. It can, through demand of the Infinite, be made in time to act in perfect accord with the spirit. The Supreme Power can and will send us a supreme love for the body. That love we need to have. Not to love one's body is not to love one expression of the Infinite Mind.

We are not implying that you "ought" to have more love for your body, or that you "ought" in any respect to do or act differently from your deeds, acts and thoughts as they are at present. "Ought" is a word and idea regarding others that we have nothing to do with. There is no reason in saying to a blind man "you ought to see." There is no more reason in saying to anyone "you ought not to have this or that defect of character." Whatever our mental condition may be at present, we must act out.

A man cannot of his individual self put an atom more of the element of love in himself than he now has. Only the Infinite Mind can do that. Whatever of error in character and belief we have to-day, we shall act out to-day in thought or deed. But we need not always have that mind.

The Overruling Mind will, as we demand, give us new minds, new truths, new beliefs, and as these supplant and drive out old errors, there will come corresponding changes for the better, in both mind and body. And these ever improving changes have no end. There is to these changes but one gate and one road. That gate and road lies in an unceasing demand of the Infinite to perfect us in its way.

"There is a natural body, and there is a spiritual body." In other words, we have a body of physical element which can be seen and felt, and we have another body (the spiritual), intangible to our physical senses. When we are able to love, cherish and admire our physical body as one piece of God's handiwork, we are putting that higher love element not only into that physical body, but also into the spiritual body. We cannot of ourselves make this quality of love. It can come to us only through demand of the Infinite. It is not vanity or that lower pride, which values more whatever effect its own grace and beauty may have on others than it values that grace and beauty. The higher love for the body will attend as carefully to its external adornment in the solitude of the forest as it would in the crowded city. It will no more debase itself by any vulgar act in privacy than it would before a multitude.

If God gives one personal beauty and symmetry in physical proportions, should not he or she thus favoured with a gift from the Supreme, admire it? Is it vanity to love and admire and seek to improve and increase any talent we may find in ourselves? If God made man and woman " in His own image," is it an image to be loved and admired, or regarded with hatred and distrust? Why, the religious belief of less than a hundred years ago has actually courted ugliness, and implied that it was more creditable than beauty. Had some of those solemn-visaged professors been delegated to make an angel after their own ideal, they would have turned out a duplicate of themselves.

The Infinite, as we demand, will give us wisdom and light to know what we owe to ourselves. People have been over-ridden with the idea of the " duties " they owed to parent, relative, or friend.

The road to heaven has been marked out as one full of sacrifice and self-denial for the sake of others, and with little good or pleasure for self.

If Christ should be taken as an example in this respect, we find a very different course implied. When charged with lack of attention for his mother he asks, " Who is my mother?" When the young man pleads as an excuse for not immediately following Christ, that filial duty demanded he should go and bury his father, the Messenger of a new and higher law said, "Let the dead bury their dead.' In other words, " if father, or mother, or sister, or brother, are steeped in a life-long course of trespass and sin—if their lives have been one continual violation of spiritual law, bringing the inevitable penalty of disease and pain—if they are hardened and fossilized in their false beliefs, and regard your opinions as visionary and impractical, you cannot, without injury, have fellowship with them. If you pretend for sake of peace to agree with them, you are living a lie, and when you act or live a lie you materialize it and put it in your body, whe e it is a breeder of pain and unrest. If others cannot see the law of life as clearly as you, and in their blindness go stumbling on and filling themselves with decay and disease, it is not in the line of the highest justice that you should be called on to nurse them every time they are sick, to absorb their sick and unhealthy thought, to give them your life and vitality (for this you do when you think much of any one), and to be dragged down with them. You are not responsible for their blindness. Nor can you open their eyes and make them see what is proven to you to be truth. Only the Infinite can do that. You do those who are in this lower and material current of thought no real good in ministering to them physically or spiritually. You may, having the stronger mind, bolster them up for a time, and throwing your mind in theirs give them your strength, but you cannot do this always, and when your influence is removed, as some time it must be, they will fall back to their old condition. What then have you accomplished? You have taken so much force out of yourself that you owed to yourself, and to have taught them to depend on you and not on what every one must learn to depend—the Supreme Power. Let the dead then who are still above ground bury their dead. Give them a thought and wish for their highest welfare whenever you do think of them, and leave them in God's care.

But when you put the Higher Love into yourself —when you reserve your forces to raise yourself higher in the scale of being—when it is your aim and unceasing silent prayer to be raised out of the current of the lower and material thought into that spiritual condition beyond the reach of physical disease—when you aspire to have every sense and faculty refined and strengthened beyond the present lot of mortals—when you begin to realize through the proofs coming to you that these are possibilities, then you are a real benefit to everyone. You are then proving a law. You are showing that there is a road out of the ills which afflict humanity, and when others, seeing these things evidenced in your life, ask how you obtain them, you can reply, "I have grown, and am ever growing into a higher and happier condition of mind and body through knowledge of a law, and that law is as much for you to live by as for me." You may be able to say, " I believe in the existence of the Great Overruling Power which will show me ever the happier way of life as I demand wisdom of that Power. I had little faith in the existence of that Power at first, but I was prompted to pray or demand ability to see its reality. Now my faith in its reality is growing firmer."

To throw our whole being, care, and thought into the welfare of others, no matter who they may be, without first asking of the Supreme if it be the wisest thing to do is a sin, for it is an endeavour to use the forces given us by that Power as we think best. The result is damage to self and a great lessening of ability to do real good to others.

Between the Supreme Mind and ourselves there will exist a love which is at once a love of ourselves and a love of that Mind. We must love what we draw from it, since what we draw and make part of self is drawn from God and is a part of God. Every thought we give to the Supreme Wisdom enriches us and directs us in the lasting path of happiness. Every thought we give to others not directed by that Higher Wisdom is unwisely bestowed. That Wisdom will direct our thought, love and sympathy to those on whom it can be bestowed without injury. To have our thoughts ever flowing spontaneously toward the Infinite Mind is to be one with God and a wise lover of self, as we feel ourselves more and more parts of God manifest in the flesh.

If we give sympathy and aid, material or moral, to others as they call for it, and without reservation or judgment, people will take all we have to give and come open-mouthed for more. They will keep this up until we are exhausted.

No outsider will put a limit to your giving. You must do that yourself. What is called "generous impulse" is sometimes another name for extravagance and injustice to somebody. Those who fling money to servitors and overpay largely for trifling services often owe that money to others, or they may owe it to themselves. In the real spiritual domain of being, we find this injustice perpetrated on a still larger scale. Sympathetic natures sometimes give their whole lives to others. Giving thus their life and force to others becomes a fixed habit. They become unable to restrain or control their sympathy.

It overflows at everybody's call. They deprive themselves of things really needed and take up with the poorest in order to satisfy a mania for the squandering of time, force, effort, and thought on others. A widely spread idea prevails that we can never give too much or do too much for others. It argues that salvation is more readily attained by such reckless expenditure of self than in any other way. No matter how barren it makes our lives— no matter how much we deprive ourselves, it is to be made up to us ten-fold in time.

We deem this a great mistake. We believe there is a Divine Economy which orders that when we give even of our thought, we give only as much as will really benefit others. Reckless prodigality throws dollars to children when cents would do them as much good.

Reckless prodigality of sympathy (force) often

gives ten times more to a person than that person can appropriate.

What they cannot appropriate is lost for them, and when you have sent it once out you cannot recall it.

Undoubtedly to some the idea of giving so much love to self will seem very cold, hard, and unmerciful. Still this matter may be seen in a different light, when we find that "looking out for Number One," as directed by the Infinite, is really looking out for Number Two, and is indeed the only way for permanently benefiting Number Two. The gifts conferred by the Supreme Power are "perfect gifts," and a "perfect gift" once received by us goes out and benefits many others. So soon as one person on this planet receives the "perfect gift" of immortality in the flesh, involving perfect health and freedom from all pain and disease, that gift will be contagious, for health is catching as well as disease. The corner-stone of all symmetrical growth and constant increase of mental and physical power is the reservation and care of our thought forces. This wisdom can only come as we demand it of the Supreme Power.

I am often asked "How do you know what you assert?" Or, "Have you proven these assertions to yourself?" I know what I assert to be true, because I have seen the beneficial results as regards health and condition in life proven me to an extent. Other proofs are constantly coming. But what is proven to me is really no permanently convincing proof to any other person. That kind of proof you can only get from yourself and by the exercise and growth of your share of power given you by the

Infinite. In the physical world we can safely accept the statement of a navigator who asserts his discovery of a new island. The island looks the same to every physical eye. But on the spiritual side of life spiritual things do not appear the same to all eyes. There are, so to speak, spiritual islands, and spiritual realities which one person can see, and another cannot see. You will see and get proof of these in proportion as you grow, and very possibly when you tell these things to others, they will call you a visionary, or ascribe the material proof of such growth to some material cause. In the spiritual life every person is his or her own discoverer, and you need not be grieved if your discoveries are not believed in by others. It is not your business to argue and prove them to others. It is your business to push on, find more, and increase your own individual happiness.

Christ said to those of his time, " Though one rose from the dead you would not believe him." In this respect the world has not much changed since Christ used a material body on Earth.

COSIMO is a specialty publisher of books and publications that inspire, inform and engage readers. Our mission is to offer unique books to niche audiences around the world.

COSIMO CLASSICS offers a collection of distinctive titles by the great authors and thinkers throughout the ages. At **COSIMO CLASSICS** timeless classics find a new life as affordable books, covering a variety of subjects including: *Biographies, Business, History, Mythology, Personal Development, Philosophy, Religion and Spirituality*, and much more!

COSIMO-on-DEMAND publishes books and publications for innovative authors, non-profit organizations and businesses. **COSIMO-on-DEMAND** specializes in bringing books back into print, publishing new books quickly and effectively, and making these publications available to readers around the world.

COSIMO REPORTS publishes public reports that affect your world: from global trends to the economy, and from health to geo-politics.

FOR MORE INFORMATION CONTACT US AT
INFO@COSIMOBOOKS.COM

If you are a book-lover interested in our current catalog of books.

If you are an author who wants to get published

If you represent an organization or business seeking to reach your members, donors or customers with your own books and publications

**COSIMO BOOKS ARE ALWAYS
AVAILABLE AT ONLINE BOOKSTORES**

_____ VISIT COSIMOBOOKS.COM _____
BE INSPIRED, BE INFORMED

Printed in the United States
75287LV00003B/292